PRAISE FOR *DINING AT*

"From one of the most magical places on earth comes the cookbook every guest has been waiting for. Whether or not you've stayed at Mendocino's beloved Stanford Inn, you'll be immediately transported to the seaside bed-and-breakfast with this collection of coveted recipes. Jeff and Joan Stanford have created a luxurious retreat unlike any other, and the food at The Ravens is on par with the best fine dining restaurants in the country. Now, everyone can enjoy the inn's spectacular cuisine—from the Citrus Polenta and Ravens Caesar Salad to the Seasonal Wild Mushroom Crepe and my favorite dessert of all time, the Pecan Torte. If heaven exists in the form of a cookbook, this is it."

—COLLEEN HOLLAND, PUBLISHER OF *VegNews* MAGAZINE

"Finally, something different in the world of vegan cookbooks! While 30-minute weeknight meals have their place, sometimes you just want to roll up your sleeves and cook the comforting, delicious kind of food you'd get at a bed-and-breakfast. For that, *Dining at The Ravens* delivers—from homemade breads, to luxurious sauces and mains, to brunches you'll want to share with friends—it's all here. And it's all healthy, whole, and compassionate. This is the kind of cooking I thought I'd never get to do again."

—MATT FRAZIER, VEGAN ULTRAMARATHONER AND AUTHOR OF *NO MEAT ATHLETE*

"The recipes in *Dining at The Ravens* are a perfect mirror to the experience of staying at Stanford Inn: comforting, familiar, magical, and delightfully surprising. The tantalizing array of tastes showcased in this book are diverse enough to seduce the most seasoned gourmand, yet simple and approachable enough to be enjoyed by new fans of plant-based cuisine. If you can't make the life-changing trip to visit the inn in Mendocino, this book gives you a beautiful glimpse of the culinary genius and natural beauty there!"

—JASON WROBEL, CELEBRITY VEGAN CHEF AND HOST OF *HOW TO LIVE TO 100* ON COOKING CHANNEL

"There is no place like the Stanford Inn. Jeff and Joan have built an amazing business rooted in compassion, sustainability, and wellness, and I absolutely love visiting. This book is an extension of their ideals and vegan lifestyle, and the delicious recipes show that living this way is enjoyable and enriching."

—GENE BAUR, PRESIDENT AND COFOUNDER OF FARM SANCTUARY

"When I stayed at the Stanford Inn by the Sea, everything was breathtaking: estuaries, gardens, forests, and fireplaces. But what made it truly remarkable was the food at The Ravens. I hope that one day you too will be able to visit this extraordinary place. In the meantime, the next best thing is bringing The Ravens to your home. The recipes in this book prove that indulgence and nourishment perfectly commingle."

—JOSHUA KATCHER, ADJUNCT PROFESSOR AT PARSONS THE NEW SCHOOL, FOUNDER AND CREATIVE DIRECTOR OF BRAVEGENTLEMAN.COM, AND EDITOR OF THEDISCERNINGBRUTE.COM

DINING AT THE RAVENS

DINING AT THE RAVENS

Over 150 Nourishing Vegan Recipes from the Stanford Inn by the Sea

Jeff and Joan Stanford

BENBELLA BOOKS, INC.
DALLAS, TX

BenBella

BenBella Books, Inc.
10300 N. Central Expressway
Suite #530
Dallas, TX 75231
www.benbellabooks.com
Send feedback to feedback@benbellabooks.com

Library of Congress Cataloging-in-Publication Data:
Stanford, Jeff, 1946-
  Dining at The Ravens : over 150 nourishing vegan recipes from the Stanford Inn by the sea / Jeff and Joan Stanford.
    pages cm
  Includes bibliographical references and index.
   ISBN 978-1-941631-65-2 (trade paper : alk. paper)—ISBN 978-1-941631-66-9 (ebook) 1. Vegan cooking. 2. Ravens (Restaurant) 3. Stanford Inn (Mendocino, Calif.) I. Stanford, Joan. II. Title.
   TX837.S724 2016
   641.5'636—dc23
                    2015020361

The Ravens logo artwork by Lisa Garza-Hillman and
    Kim Hillman of Inkfish Design
Photography by the Stanford Inn unless otherwise noted
Photography on pages 20, 21, 23, and 24 by Jeff Stanford
Photography on pages 5, 6, 32, and 63 by Rex Gelert
Photography on page 19 by Justin Lewis
Photography on page 29 by Christine Gustafson
Photography on pages 27, 34, 45, 75, 139, 235, and 270 by
    Daniel MacDonald / www.dmacphoto.com
Photography on pages 40, 161, and 255 by
    Brendan McGuigan
Photography on page 42 by Paul Beauchemin

Cover photography by Justin Lewis (top) and
    the Stanford Inn (bottom row)
Photography on page 16 by Sara Remington /
    sararemington.net
Editing by Heather Butterfield
Copyediting by Karen Levy
Proofreading by Kristin Vorce Duran and
    Brittney Martinez
Indexing by WordCo Indexing Services, Inc.
Cover design by Sarah Dombrowsky
Text design and composition by Kit Sweeney
Additional text composition by Aaron Edmiston

Printed in Malaysia
10 9 8 7 6 5 4 3 2 1

Distributed by Perseus Distribution
www.perseusdistribution.com

To place orders through Perseus Distribution:
Tel: (800) 343-4499 / Fax: (800) 351-5073 / E-mail: orderentry@perseusbooks.com

Significant discounts for bulk sales are available.
Please contact Glenn Yeffeth at glenn@benbellabooks.com or (214) 750-3628.

To our parents, Jean and Gordon Horne and
Peggy and Rolf Stanford, who in their different ways
showed us the way; to Kate and Alex, our children,
who are constant reminders of the future; and to all
those with the courage to act from consciousness.

CONTENTS

PROLOGUE

INNKEEPING AS A STATE OF MIND . . . A NOTE FROM JEFF AND JOAN

Jeff, Kansas, Kate, Alex, and Joan in their first home at the inn, "The Barn"

Imagine a small resort, with an inn and a restaurant, that celebrates life. One guided by the principle to serve the highest and best purposes of its guests.

The Stanford Inn is such a resort. This cookbook is an expression of a tradition of innkeeping as service that began in the late 1970s when we sought a way to live an integrated life—raising a family, working, being in nature, providing meaningful service, and continuing our education, all at a single site—much like that found on the small family farms that dominated Manitoba and Kansas, where we were raised. A series of opportunities (or lack thereof) suggested innkeeping as a contemporary approach to achieving the goal of an integrated family life and providing meaningful getaways—holidays. *Holiday* comes from the Old English *holy day*, or to our secular minds, *wholly day*—a time to rediscover one's wholeness.

Purchasing a motel—Big River Lodge, on the edge of Mendocino—as much for its location as for the potential to convert it into a bed-and-breakfast inn, and eventually a resort, we found ourselves experiencing an affinity to the land and a sensitivity to nature in remarkable ways. Loving animals, we could no longer eat them; loving gardening and plants, we eliminated the use of pesticides and herbicides and joined California Certified Organic Farmers. When we eventually expanded the inn and built additional rooms and a restaurant, we sought "green" technologies and materials, although the term *green* was not yet in vogue and LEED certification did not exist.

We opened The Ravens Restaurant first as a vegetarian restaurant to reflect our lifestyle, and then after we became vegan, our restaurant became vegan, too. Today, The Ravens features cuisine created with whole foods, setting it apart from most other vegan restaurants. Jeff's experience long ago in anthropology convinced us that we evolved eating "low-hanging fruit" and other accessible plants; that man—who evolved with the soil bacteria that are so important for digestion and the vitality of our immune systems—was and is primarily an herbivore.

Wanting to share our vision in every possible way, we created internship programs to develop professional produce gardeners as well as chefs. At The Ravens, the model for our enterprise is co-creation: there is no single chef. We oversee the kitchen, and everyone is invited to participate in the creation of new dishes and, more important, to creatively evaluate existing menu items with the underlying understanding that many cooks make a better dish.

The recipes in *Dining at The Ravens* are the result of this process. They were created and tested not only by us and our family, friends, and staff, but also by guests and diners, who have commented and advised us over the years. Our diners are who we cook for and serve and they are the final arbiters. We hope that you enjoy the dishes prepared from these recipes as much as we have enjoyed creating and serving them.

FOREWORD

COLLEEN PATRICK-GOUDREAU

Despite the fact that compassion is a guiding principle in all the world's religions and secular philosophies, and despite the fact that compassion is instilled in us by our parents and other adults in our lives, we're also taught that compassion is acceptable as long as it is selective—that is, reserved only for certain groups or species. We're taught to love our household dogs, cats, and rabbits, but we're also taught that other domesticated animals, such as pigs, cows, chickens, turkeys, and even rabbits, are here for us to eat and use as we please.

By the time we're young adults, the unconditional compassion we had for animals as children gets put to sleep in favor of the pleasure and convenience of eating burgers, milkshakes, and dismembered legs and wings. We're taught to compartmentalize animals into those we love and those we eat. Chickadees good. Chickens food. We go along our merry way, eating everything that once walked or swam or flew, until a fateful moment when we become reawakened to that unconditional compassion—when we "become vegan."

Because we live in a non-vegan world—a world that in many ways supports violence against animals—once we are awakened, we become acutely aware of all the ways in which we hurt animals in our society, and we see and feel this suffering much more keenly than when we were asleep. This can become so difficult to cope with that some people choose to go back to sleep and return to eating animals.

Alternatively, many vegans become hopeless or cynical, angry, or depressed and begin to understand how necessary it is to seek out like-minded people, to find a reprieve from all of the suffering they're reminded of on a daily basis.

The Stanford Inn provides such a respite. It is a sanctuary for the soul and a balm for the body. At the Stanford Inn, you feel a sense of belonging, a sense of safety, a sense of peace.

You are surrounded by others who speak your language. It is a haven unto itself, where no animals are harmed and where all who visit are nourished—by the surrounding aromas, sights, sounds, and cuisine.

One of the biggest misconceptions about being vegan is that it's an end in itself—that it's about being perfect or trying to attain some kind of purity certification. Nothing could be further from the truth. To me, being vegan is about doing everything we can to not hurt anyone (including ourselves). It's about doing the best we can to make the most compassionate choices. It's not about purity; it's about consistency. It's not about perfection; it's about intention.

This intention, this compassion, is reflected in everything the Stanfords do. It is infused in all the food they serve. And it is embodied in this cookbook you now hold in your hands. Whether you treat yourself to a weekend full of meals at The Ravens Restaurant or make these recipes in your own kitchen, there is something incredibly special about preparing and sharing food for which no animals are harmed for the sake of our pleasure.

When a sense of consciousness informs our actions, when our intentions reflect loving-kindness, when our thoughts turn to someone else's well-being rather than our own desires, there is no denying that something profound takes place. Recent studies even suggest that food made with kind intentions can increase pleasure and make things taste better.

In the absence of violence, there is peace. In the presence of compassion, there is joy.

That is what *Dining at The Ravens* is all about, and how fortunate we all are not only to visit the sanctuary they have built in Mendocino, California, but also to bring that sanctuary into our own homes.

May you make choices that reflect your deepest values, and may you find abundance and joy in a life lived simply so that others may simply live.

●————————————————————●

COLLEEN PATRICK-GOUDREAU'S compassionate living philosophy is propelling plant-based eating into the mainstream and forever changing how we regard animals.

A recognized expert and thought leader on the culinary, social, ethical, and practical aspects of living vegan, Colleen Patrick-Goudreau is an award-winning author of seven books, including the best-selling *The Joy of Vegan Baking*, *The Vegan Table*, *Color Me Vegan*, *Vegan's Daily Companion*, *On Being Vegan*, and *The 30-Day Vegan Challenge*. She is an acclaimed speaker and a multimedia host, beloved especially for her inspiring podcast, *Food for Thought*, which was voted Favorite Podcast by *VegNews* magazine readers. Colleen is a regular contributor to National Public Radio and has appeared on the Food Network and PBS.

PART ONE

About
the Stanford Inn
and The Ravens

A HISTORY
OF NORTH AMERICA'S
VEGAN RESORT:
THE STANFORD INN

THE VILLAGE OF MENDOCINO sits above the Pacific Ocean on headlands extending from the western edge of the redwood forest, more than an hour and a half from the nearest major highway. Just to the south of the village, Big River Lodge, as the Stanford Inn was originally known, overlooks Mendocino Bay on property that was and remains a highly energetic enclave—a sloping meadow, surrounded by forest ridges and the bay. This setting—this place—has a momentum and direction of its own. As we settled onto this land, we didn't have a clue.

Big River Lodge, 1981

We did not come to Mendocino to start an organic farm with an inn, a vegetarian and eventually vegan restaurant, and a spa. We wanted to create a showplace: a stellar resort, with an outstanding gourmet restaurant, cocktail lounge, meeting rooms, tennis courts, and a golf course: all that it takes to create a premier destination.

Our desires far exceeded our capacity to achieve them. We had no money and had only been able to purchase the inn in part because the sellers loaned us a substantial portion of the down payment. They did not want to give up their residence, which they divided from the property. With no house, we lived in one of the inn rooms that had an adjoining kitchen. Occupancy was so low that the depleted room inventory was not a problem.

With no money, we began landscaping. This we could afford: our labor, a few plants, and the major purchase of a lawn mower to cut grass after the first rains.

Big River Lodge circa 1984

Six months after we closed escrow, in the midst of gardening, Alex, our son, was born. He arrived on one of the few days in the history of our innkeeping that there were no guests. We were fully able to attend to the miracle of his birth.

We began to feel a custodial responsibility to the property, and the land seemed to respond. Joan, standing on the deck in those first few months, wished for a better ocean view. Along the old highway that cut in front of the property, 100-year-old cypresses blocked much of the view to Mendocino Bay. Shortly after Joan made her wish, on a calm, cloudless day, the cypresses began to fall onto the old highway. We later rationalized that rain must have undermined their roots. Whatever the cause, the trees granted Joan's wish. Much later, when deciding to expand and build, we were trying to figure out building placement to avoid killing trees. They, too, gave way unexpectedly, and not during storms.

Our first season came, and with additional funds borrowed from friends we began to change a motel into an inn, installing wood-burning fireplaces, paneling with real wood, and refurnishing. Jeff built and Joan ran the office, greeting guests and showing them to their rooms, all the while caring for and carrying Alex.

By the time Kate, our daughter, was born less than two years later, we had taken over another of the inn's rooms to serve as our bedroom. Kate arrived just after the holiday season. As with Alex, we were able to attend to her birth. The four of us lived in our newly expanded quarters with Toronto, our Labrador; Rivers, an Australian sheep dog; and Gimpy, Thumper, Stormy, Chessie, and Sebastian, cats who had joined us over the years.

The inn was changing, and so were we. Before coming to Mendocino, Jeff cooked and was known for barbecue and specialty dishes such as marinated seared roast leg of lamb; now he found he had no taste for meat or fish—a former fisherman and midwesterner, he had seen the suffering of a walleye pike, a chicken, and a cow. Friends asked why he no longer chose to eat meat, and he answered, "I can't ask someone to do something for me I wouldn't do for myself—slaughter an animal!" His awareness of suffering led Jeff to begin experiencing energy fields around people, animals, and plants. He saw discrete energies, devas, as moving light. Later we learned that a "line" of "earth energy" moved across the property, through the actual rooms in which we lived. In England this energy is called a ley line, and monuments such as Stonehenge, St. Michael's Mount, and other sacred sites are said to lie along these energy lines.

As we began our sixth year, we decided to "landscape" the lower part of the property. A pond sits above what is left of an orchard planted before 1900. The land had been covered with clay removed from the bottom of the pond years before, leaving a rough terrain with sparse grasses and weeds. Kris Williams, the son of the original owners, and Jeff double-dug five beds for biointensive gardens cutting through the heavy clay. Our goal was to create beautiful landscaping that also fed people. We were determined to do so without the use of pesticides, herbicides, and chemical fertilizers. We mixed

Stanford family 1986; Kate 3, Alex 5

Gardens circa 1990

the native clay with compost made from our continental breakfast food waste, garden clippings, grass cuttings, and llama and horse manure.

Gardening was challenging, and we adopted practices advocated by Machaelle Wright of the Perelandra Center for Nature Research in Virginia, and by John Jeavons in Willits, California. From Wright we learned to work with garden energies, or devas. From Jeavons we learned companion planting and intensive gardening. We set aside areas for predators and for pests. Gophers were "allowed" some beds and all of the ornamental landscaping. Every year, and sometimes several times a year, we requested that they stay out of the remainder of our vegetable beds. They did. At least, they did until Jeff forgot to ask them to stay away.

In our first year of ownership we had sought and received a coastal development permit for much of what we believed would allow us to become a premier destination. The following years we ran into one obstacle after another. Money was a problem, and frankly we were not ready. There was much yet to learn.

In 1987–88, Alex and Kate were beginning school, and after eight years living behind the office and small lobby, we built "The Barn" for animals, storage, and ourselves. Finally we could sleep on a real bed rather than the sofa bed in our living room/dining room/bedroom. We were not able to build new guest accommodations, a lobby, and a restaurant. The buildings were far too expensive, but we did manage to build a pool and a greenhouse enclosure.

The pool at the Stanford Inn, built in 1991

Jeff focused on learning more about the human energy system and we continued working with the energies on the land. We brought Dana Ecelberger into the gardens. She knew nothing about gardening and began learning as we had, from doing. She, too, became aware of our co-creative relationship with the land.

We grew in our understanding. Suddenly, and there is no better way to describe it, we became aware that to live we eat life! This was realization in its fullest sense. It wasn't joyful; it was stunning.

Many of us eat sentient life, "knowing" life: animals. By then we were "vegetarians"; however, working with plant energies, we knew that plants are aware, sentient in ways not as obvious. Eating dairy provided no refuge from killing sentient life. Dairy products are obtained through breeding, which leads inevitably to slaughtering unwanted male offspring. Dairy, nonfertile eggs, and honey—all may not demonstrate obvious sentience; however, they are the products of sentient life.

Killing is killing. As supposedly highly evolved beings, some of us argue that eating lesser-evolved animals is all right. A vegan has no reason to be righteous. Plants are life and we may not be able to identify with them as easily as a cow or horse; however, plants live, reproduce, and respond to the energies and other beings around them. Humans may consider plants lesser than animals, but this is simply animal-centric thinking.

In our growing awareness of the nature of eating, it became clear that the planet exists to be savored and enjoyed—embraced. After all, we eat it. The cost to each of us is that we are responsible for caring for it—nurturing it—so that after 1,000 years or more, it is still a lovely, healthy place for the enjoyment of others.

We slowly began to understand life in a way we never had before. A veal calf became one of the most loving of all creatures, born virtually into a cage, giving his body to become food. And we had no intention to figuratively ask a calf or any other animals, including chickens, to suffer. In the United States, more than 260 million male chicks are killed every year in the nation's hatcheries, and 40 million in British hatcheries. We could list more, but the issue is to move beyond causing suffering, and toward joy—and that movement begins in positive action, bringing intelligence and compassion into the kitchen. Plant-based whole foods are nourishing and easy to prepare. Diners leave Thanksgiving dinner at The Ravens feeling buoyed, nourished, and sensitive rather than bilious, looking for the nearest sofa on which to crash.

We know the benefits of eating a whole-food, plant-based diet go beyond reducing suffering, greenhouse gases, poverty, and the guilt that comes with "knowing better" while ignoring what we know. Many of the illnesses afflicting us are related to diet, and paying attention to what we eat is essential for health. This is not obsession; paying attention means understanding how food nourishes, how it impacts us. It is approaching diet with intelligence.

The Ravens Restaurant is our response to this realization. We opened The Ravens in 1997 as a vegetarian restaurant consistent with our lifestyle, and after we became vegan, The Ravens became vegan. We choose to make ethical, healthful cuisine created from plants, seaweed, and fungi raised or collected in the most sustainable manner possible.

At The Ravens, we choose to serve a whole-food, plant-based diet, setting us apart from most other vegan restaurants in the United States. Many vegan and vegan-friendly restaurants rely on seitan, soy protein isolates, and tofu in main courses to replace meat. Seitan is pure wheat gluten and can be flavored and then roasted, grilled, or fried and can smell like and taste like animal meats. Soy protein isolates are nearly pure soy protein, concentrating the protein and with it, phytoestrogens. Tofu is the least processed of the three but lacks fiber. A version of edamame, or soybeans, is tempeh, a fermented soy product and a whole food. We do not use seitan or soy isolates at all. We avoid using tofu in a major role of a dish, relegating it to a condiment.

We know that the plants we serve at The Ravens are living and sentient, but they are at the base of the "food chain," and eating them reduces the amount of energy required to bring food to our mouths, along with the suffering of animals. Eating plants eliminates the middle animals. And eating plants has revolutionized our farming practices. We treat each plant with respect and allow, as much as possible, each to express itself fully by coming into flower and seed. Where we can, we pick leaves, not the entire plant. As the plant begins to flower, we quit picking and allow it to go to seed. We can't always do this, but where we can, we do. The point is that it changes our relationship to plants and helps make us better farmers.

The Ravens Restaurant, more than most restaurants, is about nourishing and enhancing our sense of living. Our purpose is to demonstrate that a plant-based, whole-food diet is not only a better way to "eat the planet," but it's also an outstanding way to eat: you'll feel great, nourished—fed—by dishes rivaling those at the finest California restaurants.

As mentioned in the prologue, we are guided by the principle to serve the highest and best purposes of our guests, and this cookbook celebrates that tradition. The ingredients in this book are not so much the produce, grains, spices, tubers, gardening tips, and stories about our recipes, but also the consciousness, the nature of the awareness, that we and our staff bring not only to the creation of the dishes served at the restaurant, but also to the creation of the inn, gardens, and programs that constitute the Stanford Inn today.

ABOUT THE RESTAURANT AND HISTORIC FARM

THE NAME

The restaurant at the Stanford Inn by the Sea, The Ravens, was named for the pair of ravens who took up residence on the property in late May 1995. They were the first we ever saw here during the fifteen years we had owned the inn. The raven pair played on our heavy equipment, squawking at their images in the mirrors and rummaging through our compost piles that we later moved to make way for the restaurant.

The ravens' arrival had a greater significance for us. Earlier that spring, when visiting Jeff's dad on the Monterey Peninsula, we watched ravens on the bicycle path in New Monterey. Jeff's dad nodded toward a raven, saying he felt a special affinity for them. If he returned after death, he told us, it would be as a raven. He died six weeks later unexpectedly. The ravens joined us two weeks after that.

ORGANIC GARDENS: THE CENTERPIECE OF THE INN

"I don't think people realize what an unusual situation it is to eat food picked just hours before it arrives at their table. The food we pick in our gardens is alive with vital energy, containing more substantial amounts of valuable nutrients. On some level, I think people feel more nourished from our freshly picked organic food."

—DANA ECELBERGER, FORMER DIRECTOR OF BIG RIVER NURSERIES

We think of ourselves as a garden with an inn, rather than an inn with a garden.

More than a century ago, on the hillside rising above the cliffs forming Mendocino Bay at the mouth of Big River, Chinese gardeners rented small parcels of land to grow produce for the logging community of Mendocino. We did not know about the "China Gardens" when we purchased the land that was also the site of the Big River Lodge and today the Stanford Inn by the Sea and The Ravens Restaurant. The gardens here have been resurrected and are now Big River Nurseries, our

USDA-certified organic farm. Originally begun as a landscaping project to demonstrate the beauty of vegetable gardening, Big River Nurseries was soon growing produce for nearby restaurants and now provides organic produce, herbs, and edible flowers for the inn's gourmet vegan restaurant.

The gardens have been carefully doubly dug with raised beds to optimize square footage and reduce erosion. Planting is specifically designed to work with the natural habitat. For example, the animals, mostly deer, that would normally graze on the planted crops are provided with their own patch of food. This translates to a garden that's more in harmony and balance with nature.

Using biodynamic techniques that combine French intensive and organic methods, we raise thirty-two varieties of lettuces from seed, along with beets, chard, cabbages, spinach, radishes, carrots, strawberries, and raspberries. The garden also specializes in hard-to-find gourmet vegetables, including tah tsai mustard, edible peapods, and heirloom leeks. Planted among the vegetables are edible flowers, which are used in The Ravens kitchen as part of our signature garnish of each dish. The garden serves a dual purpose: furnishing visitors with fresh organic produce and flowers, while setting a thriving example of environmentally sound farming practices.

Working in the garden provides an opportunity to get to know plants in their habitat, deepening our connection with them and enhancing their use in the kitchen. We recommend anyone inspired to cook spend time in the garden.

The garden serves as a muse for the unique restaurant it supports. On any given day, an herb that excites a cook sparks inspiration for that evening's special soup or entrée. The connection our cooks have to the food translates into a more creative approach to vegan cuisine, allowing our guests to experience meals that exceed their expectations.

THE MISSION OF THE RAVENS

Our mission is to provide healthy, organic cuisine that rivals the finest Northern California restaurants. We feel that this is the path of least resistance to demonstrate that healthy and satisfying food, produced and cooked with a lighter touch on our environment, can be a wonderful experience. It is our mission to "seduce" those often suspicious of veganism by continuing to build on our reputation as an outstanding restaurant within a highly rated inn.

All food wastes are composted. All other waste is recycled to the greatest extent possible.

We are committed to reducing our impact on the environment, and we support sustainable agriculture through our purchases and practices. Produce is organic, some produced by our USDA-certified organic farm—Big River Nurseries. Our dishes are predominately plant-based whole foods, produced without dairy or egg or other animal products. We use only the freshest organic fats, such as olive oil or expeller-pressed oils, and minimize their use as well.

In the kitchen, our mission is to ensure that our staff works co-creatively and cooperatively to

Left to right: Florentino Valerio, Sadhana Wysteria Berkow, Victor Martinez, Carson LaRoche, Francisco Luna, and Joel Camacho

Left to right: Cesar Genaro Rangel Rivera, Luis Alberto Navarro, Santos Perdomo Leiva, and Ubaldo Salazar Meraz (Not pictured: Gustavo Martinez and Jesus Antonio Zavala)

produce outstanding cuisine with seasonal organic foods. We eschew titles, preferring, instead, that each person see him or herself as a member of a team, which relies on all members' creative input to produce outstanding vegan cuisine for you. Many are graduates of the Natural Gourmet Institute in New York City or Le Cordon Bleu schools found throughout the country. We provide internships for student chefs to help fulfill their requirements for graduation. Many interns have graduated to become members of our staff.

THE PHILOSOPHY OF THIS COOKBOOK

LIVING A CONSCIOUS LIFE literally begins in the kitchen. However, it is in the kitchen and its stand-in, the restaurant, that we tend to be the least conscious. In particular, it is in the kitchen and restaurant where many of us choose to forget that every decision regarding what we eat impacts other lives.

Most of us do not want to know where our food comes from and how it gets to us. We eat out of habit. We make food our parents made, order food we have ordered before. We only think about the origin and nature of our food when we are appalled by the diets of others: some Asians eat dogs; some Africans eat monkeys; some South Americans eat guinea pigs. "Ugh!" We shudder when we think of eating dogs, yet most of us eat cattle, pigs, and a variety of birds and wild animals. In the United States alone, 9 billion animals are slaughtered every year.

What is the difference between our habits and those of other nationalities? There is none! Some Koreans may eat freshly slaughtered puppies at their local restaurants; we eat lobsters boiled from their tank. We eat cattle, which are sacred in much of India and allowed to roam freely there. We have no moral advantage: even vegans eat life to live. The idea of eating a dog shocks and awakens us to the true nature of eating: we eat life. And because it is life, it is honored by our proper use of it as food when we

* *properly, sustainably grow our food or purchase such food;*
* *provide food to the kitchen in the most conscious manner possible;*
* *waste little, and recycle and compost what waste there is;*
* *savor and appreciate our food;*
* *and, above all, enjoy working with these foods.*

When you're shopping for ingredients for recipes, we urge you to explore your neighborhood farmers' market for organic produce, local grocers who stock organic products, or the nearest Whole Foods Market. Please support sustainable agriculture and organic production through your purchasing.

TIPS FOR COOKING SUCCESS

THE TRUTH ABOUT RECIPES

A good recipe is not in itself a formula for a successful dish. The success of a dish depends on four criteria: the quality of ingredients; the care of their preparation, such as adhering to cooking times; the presentation of the dish; and, finally and most importantly, tasting. It is this latter category, tasting, that takes a printed recipe, available to anyone, and makes it yours. Tasting is vitally important. When we have a "bad night" at The Ravens, it is almost always because we did not taste our sauces, or the seasonings in our dishes, or the texture of a component.

For some readers, *Dining at The Ravens* may be the first time they have chosen to experiment with vegan cuisine. If you are in this group, please give yourself the gift of patience. Look through the recipes and attempt those that appear more familiar. A good place to start is at the beginning of many meals—with salads and soups. Soups, particularly, will give you a sense of the range of uses for nuts, beans, and a wide variety of vegetables and fruits.

A FEW WORDS ABOUT COOKING WITH OILS

We recognize that most of our dishes can be cooked without oil. In fact, we use little or no oil when cooking at home for our family. You may well ask, then, why we include oil in our recipes here. The answer is simple: the recipes in *Dining at The Ravens* are from the restaurant and our mission is to produce predominately whole-food, plant-based dishes that rival food in the finest Northern California restaurants.

Specifically, we are creating food for palates not accustomed to a diet solely made up of whole foods. Because oils, which are not a whole food, add flavor and texture to dishes, they are a significant component of the contemporary Western diet, including haute cuisine. Restaurant food, especially dessert, is often rich and dairy-based. At The Ravens, plant oils replace animal-based products such as butter, cream, lard, and eggs, making the dishes more environmentally sustainable and ethical.

If you enjoy the flavor and texture that oil provides, choose your oil wisely. There is a substantial debate regarding the best oils for high-heat cooking, low-heat cooking, flavor, health, environmental impact, and so on. We use certified organic expeller or cold-pressed oils, which are considered the most natural. To simplify our lives, for flavor in dressings and marinades, and in low-heat cooking, we use certified organic extra-virgin olive oil. For higher temperature cooking we use certified organic sunflower oil or canola oil. Both sunflower and canola oils have high smoking points beyond which free radicals and toxic fumes are released. For baking, we use either of these oils for their neutral taste—that is, they do not add undesired flavor. Whatever oil you choose, always choose one that is certified organic.

To minimize the amount of oil used, try a certified organic spray oil. If you are sautéing and spray oil is not available, pour a small amount of oil into the pan, heat it over medium, while moving the pan to spread the oil. Once the cooking surface is coated, pour off any excess and discard before adding vegetables. These methods ensure that the amount of calories contributed by the oil is miniscule.

Here are a few tips to avoid the use of plant oils:

1. *Avoid recipes that require oil as a major component in their ingredients list (many desserts, some breads, and dressings, for example).*

2. *Use stock, water, or the vegetable's own juices for braising. Pour a small amount of stock or water into a nonstick ceramic-coated pan, place it over medium heat, and add vegetables, turning frequently. If the fluid evaporates, add more to prevent burning.*

3. *Onions can be caramelized without water or stock. Cook sliced or chopped onions over medium heat, turning every couple of minutes until their fluids evaporate and the onions brown, about 15 minutes.*

4. *When oven roasting vegetables that may dry out, such as squash or potatoes, spray water or vegetable stock on them before roasting. Alternately, you can toss the vegetables in the liquid. If roasting mushrooms, spray them with water or vegetable stock and pour a small amount of stock into their caps and roast upside down. All vegetables should be roasted on parchment paper or a silicone baking mat to help prevent sticking.*

AN ESSENTIAL PIECE OF EQUIPMENT

Most kitchens will have the equipment you need to prepare any dish in this book, with the exception of a Vitamix or Blendtec blender. These high-speed blenders will produce flour from grains, puree soups and vegetable-based sauces, make smoothies, and most importantly, convert nuts such as cashews into a creamy consistency. We often use cashew cream, which is far more healthful than dairy cream and is easy to make, replacing dairy in sauces and soups. We have absolutely no affiliation with either company, other than selling Vitamix blenders in our gift shop. We urge you to check their website at www.vitamix.com or Blendtec's at www.blendtec.com. You can also find Vitamix and Blendtec blenders for sale at stores such as Costco.

THE BEST THING ABOUT SERVING VEGAN CUISINE TO NON-VEGANS

Sid Garza-Hillman, the Stanford Inn's Nutritionist

AFTER EIGHT YEARS AT the Stanford Inn, I am still struck by this thought: Why would any non-vegan ever choose to eat at The Ravens? The answer is precisely why I love working here: namely, that we demonstrate that being vegan is mainstream, accessible, easy, and most of all, fun.

Most of our guests are neither vegan nor vegetarian, and for many The Ravens is their first experience dining at a fine vegan restaurant. Because of this, our menu is often a conversation starter—a conversation I love to have. I spend a couple of nights at The Ravens each week, ensuring that our presentation and flavors are consistent, and also checking in with guests about their experience. I receive a number of questions, such as why Joan and Jeff decided to open a vegetarian restaurant, when and why they transitioned the cuisine to vegan, how the heck we pull off awesomely creamy soups without cream, and the ubiquitous and most popular question, "Where's the protein?"

The stories in this cookbook explain the backdrop to Joan and Jeff's decisions with regard to both The Ravens and the entire Stanford Inn. Their decisions about the food we serve are based in compassion and *actual* environmental sustainability. Serving plants satisfies both fronts, and serving plants as close to their original state as possible requires even less energy and natural resources than do refined/processed plants. The beautiful truth is that the more environmentally friendly and ethical a food is, the healthier it is for our bodies. It's a trifecta of cool, and the reason I love being the Stanford Inn's nutritionist.

We strive to show how easy and fun veganism can be, first because, well, it is, but also because there exists a huge amount of fear around food, as evidenced by the ever-present protein question. The fact is that whole plants are abundant in protein, and protein deficiencies (in addition to carbohydrate

and fat deficiencies, for that matter) are virtually impossible if people are consuming *enough* calories to do what they do—e.g., exercising, thinking, working, and so on. I explain basic nutrition using a gift box analogy. Picture all foods as gift boxes, with the macronutrients (i.e., calories—protein, fat, carbohydrates) as the wrapping paper on the outside of the box, and the micronutrients (vitamins, minerals, phytochemicals, antioxidants, plus fiber and water) as what is inside the box. The healthier the food, the heavier the box. Refined plants (oil, white sugar, white flour, seitan) and animal foods (flesh and dairy) are light boxes. Whole grains, beans, and seeds on up to whole fruits and vegetables are heavy boxes. The higher proportion of micronutrients that come in heavy box foods enables our bodies to burn calories more efficiently and with less stress. So instead of being primarily concerned with protein, fat, and carbohydrates, we should be asking *what comes with* our protein, fat, and carbohydrates.

In the modern world we are bombarded with ad campaigns; the perceived supreme importance of protein is frankly the result of extremely successful campaigns by the California Milk Processor Board and the National Livestock and Beef Board's Beef Industry Council. It's not that we don't need protein, but rather we need heavy box versions of *all* the types of calories. So common is the fear of not getting enough protein that *The Discerning Brute*'s Joshua Katcher and I co-coined the term *protedefiphobia*—the irrational fear of protein deficiency. A tongue-in-cheek endeavor to be sure, but again, we are trying to bring a little humor into the picture—to help people be *less* afraid, not more afraid. Showing people that putting mostly heavy box foods into their bodies is a gift, a source of joy, and a "lightening of the load" that provides a much-needed balance to the abundance of stress most of us face every day.

My hope is that the cookbook you hold in your hands adds pleasure to your life. I love food as much as the next person, but I *really* love food that not only tastes amazing but also reflects my values and ethics. Becoming 100 percent plant-based more than twelve years ago with my wife, and with her, raising a vegan family, has been nothing but a positive experience. Enjoy these recipes, come visit us, and feel free to ask any questions you might have. I'm ready for you!

———————•——————————————————•———————

SID GARZA-HILLMAN, the Small Step Advocate™, is the author of *Approaching the Natural: A Health Manifesto*, host of the *Approaching the Natural* podcast, and host of his YouTube channel. He graduated from UCLA with a BA in philosophy, and is a speaker, certified nutritionist, and health coach, working with private clients all over the world. He is also the nutritionist and programs director at the Stanford Inn's Wellness Center. Sid lives on California's Mendocino coast with his wife and three children, and has completed both 50K and fifty-mile ultramarathons.

PART TWO

The Recipes

MORNING FOOD

Breakfast at The Ravens is popular among locals and inn guests alike. For those guests who have not stayed with us before, breakfast may be their first direct experience of what constitutes vegan fare.

Breakfast at The Ravens is an expression of mindfulness. Most of the dishes are made from whole plants and use very little processed ingredients, with the exception of tofu, which serves as a substitute for eggs and has half the calories, less than a third of the fat, and none of the cholesterol that eggs contain.

Our menu boasts a wonderful and diverse selection of hearty and healthful meals, and our breakfast entrées can be served for lunch or dinner as well.

CITRUS POLENTA WITH BRAISED GARDEN GREENS AND A CREAMY TOASTED CASHEW SAUCE

8-12 SERVINGS

One of our most popular breakfast entrées was inspired by our desire to provide high-quality, exciting vegan dishes; this dish allows us to use freshly harvested greens from our gardens. Creating our citrus polenta was probably our first demonstration of collaborative effort; we thank Domenica Catelli, Janie Blake, and Porsche Combash for helping us first demonstrate what a cooperative co-creative kitchen is all about.

Citrus polenta can be served not only at breakfast, but as a lunch or dinner entrée as well. The braised greens with cashew sauce can serve as a side dish at dinner or lunch. You might try the cashew sauce on marinated grilled tofu or on vegetables such as asparagus and broccoli. It adds protein and high-quality fat to any dish.

FOR THE POLENTA

1½ cups freshly squeezed grapefruit juice

½ cup freshly squeezed orange juice

Zest of 2 oranges

Zest of 1 lemon

Zest of 1 lime

1 cup polenta

2 cups water

1 teaspoon salt

FOR THE GREENS AND SERVING

1 tablespoon olive oil

1 clove garlic, minced

1 bunch (about ½ pound) of tender kale, collards, or Swiss chard, cleaned

¼ cup Braising Sauce (page 76)

Pinch of red pepper flakes (optional)

1½ cups Cashew Sauce (page 80)

Toasted cashews, for garnish

For the Polenta

1. Bring juices and zests to a low boil in a medium-heavy saucepan.
2. Lower the heat and whisk in polenta in a slow, steady stream.
3. Add water and salt. Whisk continuously to avoid lumps and until all liquid is absorbed.
4. Cook polenta over very low heat, stirring every 10 minutes, until the cornmeal loses its raw flavor and crunchy texture.
5. Pour the polenta into a 10-inch greased cake pan and allow to cool.

   Note: Polenta can be made a day ahead and stored covered in the refrigerator.

For the Greens and Serving

1. In a medium sauté pan, heat olive oil over medium heat and add garlic. Sauté for 1 minute and add the greens. Continue to sauté greens until their color begins to darken and intensify.
2. Pour in the Braising Sauce and red pepper flakes and continue to cook until greens are tender.
3. Cut the polenta into thin slices. Lightly brown the polenta and heat through thoroughly in a medium nonstick sauté pan.
4. Pour a thin layer of heated Cashew Sauce on a plate. Arrange the polenta and place greens on top. Garnish with toasted cashews.

RAVENS FRITTATA AND QUICHE

8 SERVINGS

Before the restaurant opened, Jeff prepared quiches and frittatas with a variety of ingredients for the inn's breakfast buffet. One of the favorites was filled with onions, roasted red peppers, artichoke hearts, and sliced cooked potatoes, creating a robust single-dish breakfast. Below is a simplified version.

This recipe features tofu for those wanting an eggy consistency. Both the frittata and the quiche were popular dishes and are occasionally requested for receptions.

We recommend baking a thinner frittata—about ½ inch. It makes the frittata easier to reheat. Note that the filling is the same for both the frittata and the quiche. Simply make the vegetable filling, then the frittata batter or quiche crust depending on which dish you'd prefer.

FOR THE VEGETABLE FILLING

2 scallions, thinly sliced

½ white onion

2 teaspoons diced fresh garlic

1 teaspoon salt

½ teaspoon red pepper flakes

¼ cup white wine

1 cup sliced cremini mushrooms

1 cup uncooked spinach

1 cup seasonal vegetable of your choice (sun-dried tomatoes, zucchini, or broccoli)

FOR THE FRITTATA

1 pound firm tofu

2 tablespoons nutritional yeast

1 tablespoon salt

2 teaspoons turmeric

¼ cup plain soymilk

Juice of 1 lemon

½ cup olive oil

FOR THE QUICHE

2 cups organic unbleached all-purpose flour (more if needed)

1 teaspoon sea salt

1 teaspoon evaporated cane juice

¾ cup expeller-pressed high-oleic safflower, sunflower, or canola oil

½ cup water

¼ cup cold, dry white wine

For the Vegetable Filling

1. Sauté scallions, onion, garlic, salt, and red pepper flakes until tender. Deglaze pan with white wine.
2. Stir in mushrooms, spinach, and seasonal vegetables and cook until soft.

For the Frittata

1. Preheat oven to 350 degrees.
2. Combine all ingredients except olive oil in a food processor. Process, drizzling olive oil into the mixture for a smooth consistency.
3. Mix softened vegetable mixture with frittata batter.
4. Pour into a shallow pan sprayed with cooking oil (about ½ inch deep) and bake for 35–40 minutes until golden.

5. Let stand 30 minutes before serving.

   Note: Frittata can be refrigerated and heated per serving either on a skillet or in a hot oven.

For the Quiche

1. In a medium bowl or a food processor fitted with the metal blade, add the flour, salt, and evaporated cane juice. Pulse to mix.
2. With the food processor on, slowly add the liquids and mix until the dough comes together and forms a ball. If ball doesn't form, you may need to add up to a cup of additional flour.
3. Wrap the dough in plastic wrap and refrigerate for 1–2 hours or until ready to use.
4. Preheat oven to 350 degrees.
5. Roll out the chilled dough to thick circle about ¼ inch thick and line a 9-inch pie pan with it. Fill the pie crust with the softened vegetable mixture.
6. Bake for 35–40 minutes until golden.
7. Let sit 30 minutes before serving.

   Note: This quiche can easily be reheated if you'd like to make it ahead of serving.

LIVE SCRAMBLE

2 SERVINGS

A favorite of the raw crowd, this recipe is rich in essential fats and protein from the almonds and sunflower seeds. It is a heavier breakfast than a rich complex carbohydrate breakfast, such as our personal favorite, oatmeal porridge. We are noting this because we believe strongly that we should keep food simple and satisfying.

Our Live Scramble is best served as a side for brunch rather than a main course. When we have leftover Live Scramble, Jeff refrigerates it and eats it for lunch.

½ cup almonds, soaked for 4–6 hours and drained

½ cup sunflower seeds

1½ teaspoons turmeric

1 teaspoon cumin

¼ cup water

½ cup chiffonade spinach (sliced into thin strips)

1 tomato, diced small

2 tablespoons diced onion

2 tablespoons minced cilantro

Salt to taste

1. Combine soaked almonds and sunflower seeds in a food processor and process until coarsely ground.
2. Add turmeric, cumin, and water and process into a chunky scramble. Transfer mixture to a large bowl.
3. Fold in spinach, tomato, onion, and cilantro, and add salt to taste. Serve.

STANFORD PORTOBELLO AND STANFORD FLORENTINE

2 SERVINGS

When we opened The Ravens for breakfast, we wanted the food to be memorable and so created versions of eggs Florentine and eggs Benedict—two fantastic breakfast and brunch dishes. These are traditionally served on English muffins and they can also be served on toast. Commercial vegan English muffins are available from Rudi's Organic Bakery.

FOR THE STANFORD PORTOBELLO

1 portobello mushroom, stem removed, thinly sliced

1 tablespoon olive oil

½ teaspoon balsamic vinegar

Freshly ground pepper

FOR THE STANFORD FLORENTINE

2 cups cooked spinach

FOR THE ASSEMBLY

2 English muffins or 4 slices of bread

½ pound firm tofu, pressed, crumbled, and heated

1 cup Hollandaise Sauce (page 81) or Ravens Lemon Tahini Sauce (page 82)

Finely chopped parsley, for garnish

For the Stanford Portobello

1. Preheat oven to 350 degrees.
2. Place sliced portobello mushroom on a baking sheet. Drizzle with olive oil and balsamic vinegar. Sprinkle with freshly ground pepper and bake for 12 minutes.

For the Stanford Florentine

1. Heat the cooked spinach.

For the Assembly

1. Toast sliced English muffins or bread.
2. On each English muffin half or slice of toast, place half the portobello or spinach, half the heated tofu, and your choice of either ½ cup Hollandaise Sauce or Lemon Tahini Sauce.
3. Sprinkle with parsley and serve warm.

STANFORD RANCHERO AND SANTA FE BURRITO

1 SERVING

To make a menu more interesting, a chef will often take the same ingredients and use them in a slightly different way. The result is an expanded menu and less preparation time in the kitchen. The Stanford Ranchero and the Santa Fe Burrito are two such menu items. The difference between the two: two small blue or yellow corn tortillas versus a whole wheat tortilla!

The beauty of the ranchero and burrito is that they are built around our black beans and fantastic salsas inspired by Jayne Blake. Jayne managed the morning kitchen and helped out in the gardens until opening her own restaurant.

---

2 small blue or yellow corn tortillas (for the Stanford Ranchero) or 1 large whole wheat tortilla (for the Santa Fe Burrito) per serving

½ cup Stanford Inn Black Beans (page 268) or pinto beans, if you prefer

½ cup Mexican-Spiced Tofu Scramble (page 58)

1 tablespoon Chipotle Sauce (page 97)

2 tablespoons Salsa Cruda (page 87)

¼ cup grated Ravens Vegan Cashew Cheese (page 259; optional)

Standard Sour Crème, for garnish (page 262)

1. In a medium nonstick frying pan, heat either 2 small tortillas or 1 large.
2. In separate containers, heat the black beans, tofu, Chipotle Sauce, and Salsa Cruda.
3. If making the Stanford Ranchero, on each warm tortilla, add black beans, cashew cheese, tofu scramble, Chipotle Sauce, and Salsa Cruda.
4. If making the Stanford Burrito, simply layer the ingredients onto the center of a whole wheat tortilla, making sure that you cover only the center half of the tortilla to provide enough free tortilla to fold.
5. Top with sour crème and serve.

GARDEN SCRAMBLE

4–6 SERVINGS

The Garden Scramble is our most popular morning dish. It features our garden greens along with organic produce not as easily grown here in quantity. This recipe also features tofu, our original egg replacement. We add turmeric to make the tofu yellow. It is also chock-full of antioxidants that provide protection against Alzheimer's disease. Today we serve the scramble with a choice of quinoa or tempeh as well as tofu. Much of the flavor is derived from the same Braising Sauce used for the greens in the Citrus Polenta with Braised Garden Greens and a Creamy Toasted Cashew Sauce (page 46). Vegetables used should reflect the season.

---

1 pound extra-firm or firm tofu, drained and pressed (see note)

½ teaspoon turmeric

1 tablespoon olive oil

1 clove garlic, finely chopped

Pinch of red pepper flakes

1 cup sliced cremini mushrooms

½ cup thinly bias-sliced carrots

½ cup shredded purple cabbage

½ cup julienned red bell pepper

½ cup cauliflower florets

½ cup broccoli florets

1 medium red onion, sliced into half-moons

8 ounces Swiss chard, cleaned and torn into small pieces

¼ cup Braising Sauce (page 76)

1. In a medium bowl, crumble tofu. Add turmeric and mix with tofu.
2. In a medium sauté pan, heat olive oil over medium heat and quickly sauté garlic (for about 30 seconds).
3. Add red pepper flakes, mushrooms, carrots, cabbage, red bell pepper, cauliflower, broccoli, and onion. Sauté until vegetables are tender.
4. Add the greens. When they begin to wilt, add Braising Sauce. Allow sauce to heat through.
5. Quickly add tofu mixture and gently turn into the greens, heating it through. Serve.

Tofu Note: Wrap tofu in a paper towel and press firmly to remove excess water. Keep wrapped for at least 1 hour for best results, or up to 24 hours.

RAVENS CHILAQUILES

4–6 SERVINGS

When Sid Garza-Hillman, the Stanford Inn's nutritionist, moved to Mendocino, he looked everywhere for his favorite breakfast dish, chilaquiles. He couldn't find it. Instead, he created it on his own, using components from other breakfast dishes. There are four primary components to the dish: tortilla strips soaked in Ravens Enchilada Sauce, refried beans, Mexican Rice, and tofu-spinach scramble. Combined, they're even better than their parts!

FOR THE ENCHILADA SAUCE-COATED TORTILLA STRIPS

6 organic corn tortillas, cut into ½-inch strips

Organic oil spray

Salt to taste

2 cups Ravens Enchilada Sauce (page 98)

¼ cup shredded Ravens Vegan Cashew Cheese (page 259)

FOR THE MEXICAN-SPICED TOFU SCRAMBLE AND ASSEMBLY

1 yellow onion, finely diced

1 tablespoon minced garlic

1 tablespoon olive oil

2 pounds firm tofu, crumbled

¼ cup nutritional yeast

1 tablespoon salt

1 tablespoon turmeric

2 teaspoons black pepper

½ teaspoon chili powder

½ teaspoon ground cumin

1 cup unsweetened soymilk

Juice of 1 lemon

2 cups spinach

2 cups Mexican Rice, warmed (page 268)

2 cups "Refried" Pinto Beans, warmed (page 269)

1 cup Salsa Cruda (page 87)

For the Enchilada Sauce-Coated Tortilla Strips

1. Preheat oven to 350 degrees.
2. Lightly spray tortilla strips with oil and sprinkle with a small amount of salt.
3. Arrange strips in a single layer on a baking sheet, and toast in the oven until golden, about 10 minutes.
4. Remove from the oven, and toss in bowl with Ravens Enchilada Sauce.
5. Place mixture in a 9 x 9-inch heatproof dish.
6. Warm cashew cheese and sprinkle on top of chip and enchilada sauce mixture.
7. Place chips in the oven for about 5 minutes, or until warm.

For the Mexican-Spiced Tofu Scramble and Assembly

1. In a medium pot, sauté onion and garlic in olive oil over medium heat until soft.
2. Add the tofu, nutritional yeast, salt, turmeric, pepper, chili powder, cumin, soymilk, and lemon juice, and cook for 5–10 minutes, until flavors have blended and the tofu has cooked a bit. Taste for seasonings and add salt and pepper as desired.
3. For a crisped tofu scramble, spread the mixture on a baking sheet and heat under the broiler, or in an oven at 500 degrees for 3 minutes.
4. Place spiced tofu mixture and spinach in a sauté pan and heat over medium heat, tossing until spinach is wilted.
5. For each serving, place ½ cup of Mexican Rice, ½ cup of "Refried" Pinto Beans, 1 cup of enchilada sauce–coated tortilla strips, and ½ cup of tofu and spinach scramble mixture on a plate. Serve with side of Salsa Cruda.

Note: The Mexican-spiced tofu can also stand on its own or be served with rancheros or burritos, mixed with braised vegetables, or, as our staff prefers, mixed with fresh, sautéed jalapeños.

BRAISED VEGETABLES MORNING STYLE

When The Ravens first opened for breakfast, Jeff assisted the servers and usually missed the meal. After service, around lunchtime, he'd go into the kitchen, chop some vegetables, and cook them with Braising Sauce. Jeff's lunch is now a side or main breakfast course at the restaurant.

This dish receives its flavor from the Braising Sauce, but Jeff often enhances it further by adding small cubes of tempeh or tofu to the garlic and onions, or serves the veggies over quinoa. Sometimes we sprinkle peanuts or cashew pieces onto the cooked veggies. The veggies are amazing and nutritionally dense on their own.

1 tablespoon olive oil

1 medium white onion, chopped

1 clove garlic, minced

1 cup chopped broccoli

1 cup chopped cauliflower

½ cup coarsely chopped red or green pepper

½ cup chopped red or green cabbage

1 large carrot, cut into ⅛-inch slices

Pinch of red pepper flakes

½ cup Braising Sauce (page 76)

1. In a large sauté pan, heat olive oil over medium heat and add onion and garlic.
2. Sauté for 1 minute, then add remaining vegetables and red pepper flakes, tossing occasionally.
3. When the broccoli begins to brighten, pour in the Braising Sauce, toss vegetables to coat, reduce heat, and cover pan.
4. Toss vegetables again after 5 minutes, and replenish Braising Sauce if needed. The vegetables should be lightly coated with the sauce. Continue to cook until tender, another 5 minutes.
5. Serve alone or with steamed brown rice or quinoa.

STANFORD INN ENCHILADAS

MAKES 4 ENCHILADAS, OR 2 SERVINGS

This is a relatively simple dish made up of organic corn tortillas steeped in Chipotle Sauce, rolled and filled with quinoa (the staple of the Incans) and steamed spinach, and topped with Salsa Cruda. Steamed spinach offers much of the same consistency as melted cheese.

---

2 cups Chipotle Sauce (page 97)

4 organic corn tortillas

1 cup warm, cooked quinoa

2 cups fresh spinach, steamed

½ cup Salsa Cruda (page 87)

1. Bring Chipotle Sauce close to a boil in a skillet. Place tortillas one at time into Chipotle Sauce, turning to coat completely. Leave in skillet until soaked, about 3 minutes.
2. Remove tortillas and lay flat on a plate. Place 4 tablespoons of quinoa along the center of each tortilla, followed by a spinach layer. Create a roll by folding one side of the tortilla over the spinach and quinoa, then rolling over the other side to form a flap.
3. Place 2 filled tortillas side by side on a plate. If the tortillas are not "saucy" enough, sparingly spoon on a small amount of additional Chipotle Sauce.
4. Finish the enchiladas by topping with Salsa Cruda (about a ¼ cup over 2 enchiladas).

BREADS & BAKED GOODS

Over the years, we have moved away from heavy breads. We look at ordinary wheat breads more as condiments than substantive parts of a meal. At home, we eat bread only as a treat and at The Ravens, we no longer automatically place bread on diners' tables: it's available only by request.

The breads here are basic and tasty. At the restaurant, our Focaccia Buns (page 68) are our house bread. You'll find that recipe here plus our Flatbread, which doubles as pizza crust and sandwich bread (page 70), along with a few past favorites. And here, too, are two of our most requested recipes—The Stanford Inn by the Sea Famous Scones (page 72) and our Classic Breakfast Muffins (page 74).

RUSTIC BREAD

MAKES 2 LOAVES

One of our favorite breads, this recipe was created particularly for dipping into olive oil. It is satisfyingly crusty, with a light and airy interior. It is free form, embodying the character of our kitchen and dining room. This bread freezes very well.

Note: We have a sourdough starter in our kitchen that we keep alive and available for regular use. If you do not have your own starter, there are recipes online, or you can purchase ready-to-go starters, which, once received, require only 12–24 hours to activate.

---

2 cups water, heated to 70 degrees (not too hot, in order to prevent killing the yeast)

2¼ cups plus 2 tablespoons white sourdough starter (make sure it's really bubbly)

1 teaspoon active dry yeast

7¾ cups unbleached bread flour , plus more for sprinkling

1 tablespoon salt

1¼ cups plus 1½ tablespoons water

3 tablespoons plain soymilk

3 tablespoons olive oil

Parchment paper

Semolina flour

1. Combine water, white sourdough starter, yeast, and unbleached bread flour in the mixing bowl of a stand mixer, and using a dough hook or dough blade mix for 6 minutes at medium speed.
2. Turn the mixer off, and allow the dough to rest for 20 minutes.
3. Add salt and mix for 2 minutes, scraping down the sides of the bowl as necessary.
4. In a separate bowl, mix water, soymilk, and olive oil together. Slowly add to the dough with the mixer running, being careful to avoid sloshing. Mix on low speed until it is incorporated, and then beat on medium speed for 4 minutes. The dough will be very soft, but should pull away from the sides of the bowl.
5. Place the dough in a lightly oiled bowl and cover with plastic wrap, letting it rise at room temperature for 2–2½ hours, or until doubled in size.
6. Cut 2 pieces of parchment paper approximately 12 x 16 inches each, and place them on your work surface.
7. Heavily sprinkle the parchment with bread flour, turn out the dough onto the parchment, and shape into an oval form. Sprinkle the dough with bread flour and cover it with a towel. Allow to rest for 20 minutes.
8. Cut dough in half and place each half onto a piece of the floured parchment. You will have to scoop and allow it to stretch as you lay it in an oblong form. It should be 1–2 inches thick.
9. Dimple the dough with your fingers, being sure to press through to the parchment. Cover and let proof in a warm spot such as on top of your refrigerator, in front of a sunny window, or near your stove for approximately 2 more hours, or until dough is soft, alive, and no longer sticky.
10. During last half hour of proofing, insert a pizza stone into the oven and preheat to 450 degrees.

11. Lightly sprinkle top of bread loaves with semolina flour, then flip loaves with a peel or large spatula onto new parchment paper. Peel off the top layer of paper. Spray loaves with water for a more crusty bread, and place on the hot baking stone in your oven.

12. Bake until golden brown, approximately 30–35 minutes, spraying with water every 5 minutes after the first 15 minutes.

13. Serve after bread has cooled. If you wish to serve warm out of the oven, let cool to the touch and tear bread apart. If you would like to slice the bread, let fully cool before slicing.

BASIC SOURDOUGH BAGUETTES

MAKES 2 BAGUETTES

We slice this bread and toast it for hummus and other spreads (page 104), use it to complement salads, and serve it in our bread basket to be dipped in olive oil. It is a wonderful bread that can accompany many different recipes.

Note: We have a sourdough starter in our kitchen that we keep alive and available for regular use. If you do not have your own starter, there are recipes online, or you can purchase ready-to-go starters, which, once received, require only 12–24 hours to activate.

FOR THE SPONGE

2 tablespoons barley malt

2 tablespoons plus 2 teaspoons all-purpose flour

1 teaspoon active dry yeast

½ cup water, heated to 70 degrees (not too hot, in order to prevent killing the yeast)

FOR THE DRY AND WET INGREDIENTS

2⅓ cups high-performance bread flour

½ cup sourdough starter (see note)

4 tablespoons plus 2 teaspoons coarse whole wheat flour

1¾ teaspoons salt

2–4 tablespoons warm water

For the Sponge

1. Mix sponge ingredients and let the mixture rest for 20–30 minutes.

For the Dry and Wet Ingredients

1. Combine the dry and wet ingredients, except the warm water, in a mixing bowl. If using a food processor or stand mixer, use the dough hook.
2. Mix for 7½ minutes, slowly adding the water, until a nice dough has formed.
3. Let the dough rest for 15 minutes, then mix it or knead it another 8 minutes.
4. Transfer dough to an oiled container, turning once to ensure all sides are coated in oil.
5. Cover the dough with plastic wrap or a damp kitchen towel, and leave in a warm area until it triples in size, about 1½ hours.
6. Punch dough down and split in half. Roll each half into a long, cylindrical baguette shape.
7. Place the loaves on an oiled baking pan, cover with plastic wrap or a kitchen towel, and leave in a warm place to rest, about 45 minutes.
8. Preheat oven to 400 degrees during last half hour of second rising.
9. Bake for 15–20 minutes, or until golden brown.
10. Cool before slicing.

FOCACCIA BUNS

MAKES ABOUT 6 BUNS

A good friend told us that she would only eat at a vegetarian restaurant that served garden or black bean burgers. We thought, "Why relegate burgers only to casual dining? Let's bring them to a fine-dining setting—The Ravens!" We added a variety of burgers, including our most popular, our Barbecued Portobello (page 196). However, the burgers presented a problem—the bun. We did not want just any bun, so we created the focaccia to provide a finer and lighter bun that doesn't overwhelm the burger.

Try these buns with marinated grilled or roasted vegetables. The buns hold together and do not become mushy from the juices of the marinade.

---

4 cups water, heated to 70 degrees (not too hot, in order to prevent killing the yeast)

2 tablespoons active dry yeast

Approximately 5 cups bread flour, or 4½ cups bread flour plus ½ cup whole wheat flour

2 tablespoons salt

2 tablespoons sugar

1 tablespoon chopped fresh rosemary

2 tablespoons olive oil, plus more for brushing

1. In a large bowl or the mixing bowl of a stand mixer, combine water and yeast, and set aside until frothy, about 10 minutes.

2. Add flour, salt, sugar, rosemary, and olive oil to the yeast mixture. Knead with dough hook, dough blade, or wooden spatula for 8–10 minutes. Let dough rest for 15 minutes.

3. Roll dough out on a floured countertop to about 2 inches thick.

4. Using 5-inch round cookie cutters, cut buns (cut the rounds as close to each other as possible because you cannot not reroll this dough; it will become too tough).

5. Place circles on oiled sheet trays for the final rise. Brush with olive oil, cover, and let rise until doubled in size, 1–1½ hours.

6. Preheat oven to 350 degrees during the last half hour of rising.

7. Before baking, gently poke 5 fingers into dough to create the classic focaccia texture.

8. Bake 20–25 minutes or until very lightly browned. Toast before serving.

SEE PHOTO ON PAGE 227

WHOLE WHEAT BURGER BUNS

MAKES 16 BURGER BUNS OR 32 SLIDER BUNS

Our whole wheat bun is a more traditional bun than our focaccia. It works well with a variety of grilled vegetables, such as layers of eggplant, tomato, onion, and zucchini. To be honest, the most difficult part of making a homemade hamburger is the bun. This recipe is relatively easy, even if you are an inexperienced baker. Be sure to follow the directions carefully regarding handling and activating the yeast.

1½ tablespoons sugar

3¾ cups water, heated to 70 degrees (not too hot, in order to prevent killing the yeast)

3¾ teaspoons active dry yeast

3½ cups ultimate performer flour

2½ cups whole wheat flour

2½ cups baker's choice flour

1¼ teaspoons baking soda

1 teaspoon salt

¾ cup sunflower oil, plus more for brushing

Parchment paper

1. Mix the sugar, ½ cup of the warm water, and the yeast in a mixing bowl or the bowl of a stand mixer and set aside for about 10 minutes, or until the mixture starts to froth.
2. Sift all the flours, baking soda, and salt into the yeast mixture. Knead on low speed in a stand mixer or by hand for about 5 minutes, adding the remaining 3¼ cups warm water in 1-cup increments, until you have a dough that's smooth but slightly sticky.
3. Add the sunflower oil and continue to knead until the oil has been absorbed by the dough, about 1 more minute.
4. Place dough in an oiled bowl, turning over once to completely coat in oil. Cover with a kitchen towel, and set aside until the dough has nearly doubled in size, 1 hour.
5. Punch down the dough, and if making burger buns, divide into 16 balls that use approximately ½ cup dough for each. If making buns for sliders, make them half that size, for a total of 32 buns.
6. Shape buns into smooth balls and place at least a couple of inches apart on a lightly greased baking sheet covered with parchment paper. Flatten the tops slightly with your palms, and let the buns rise for an hour.
7. Brush or spray the tops of the buns with a little oil for a glossy look.
8. Preheat the oven to 370 degrees. Place the buns in the oven and bake 20–25 minutes. The buns will expand and touch one another.
9. Remove from the oven and transfer buns to a rack to cool before breaking them apart.
10. Slice the buns in half, and grill face-side down before serving.

FLATBREAD

MAKES ABOUT 16 FLATBREADS

This versatile dough is great for making flatbreads. We have used grilled flatbread for grilled vegetable or portobello sandwiches, as a pizza crust, and even as a rustic bread. It is not entirely whole grain, but it serves well to hold whole foods!

3–4 cups warm water

½ tablespoon sugar

3 tablespoons yeast

5 cups Giusto's Baker's Choice Flour or other unbleached flour

2 cups whole wheat flour

2 cups Giusto's Ultimate Performer Flour or other high-gluten, spring wheat flour

3 tablespoons barley malt powder (optional)

2 teaspoons salt

¼ cup olive oil

1. Combine warm water, sugar, and yeast in a large bowl. Let the mixture sit in a warm area until yeast mixture is frothy.

2. While waiting for the yeast to activate, combine flours, barley malt powder, salt, and oil in the bowl of a stand mixer. Mix well with dough hook.

3. Add the yeast mixture to the mixing bowl. Mix for 5–6 minutes. If dough is too sticky, add flour until a texture is achieved that is workable by hand.

4. Let the dough rise for 1 hour. Cover with plastic wrap or towel to avoid drafts. The dough will need to move and should not be restricted by the cover.

5. Form 16 balls from the dough using about ½ cup dough for each ball.

6. Roll out into circles ⅛ inch thick and grill on each side for 1–2 minutes before serving.

JALAPEÑO CORNBREAD

8-12 SERVINGS

The coarse polenta in this cornbread provides a grittiness that gives it a rustic texture.
It works well paired with red beans and rice, barbecue, and other spicy dishes.

---

2 tablespoons ground flaxseed

⅓ cup water

1¼ cups masa harina or yellow corn flour

1½ cups cornmeal or coarse polenta

¼ cup sugar

1 teaspoon baking powder

1 teaspoon salt

½ teaspoon baking soda

2½ cups unsweetened soymilk

¼ cup organic applesauce

¼ cup sunflower oil

2 tablespoons apple cider vinegar

½ tablespoon agave or maple syrup

3 scallions, thinly sliced on the bias

1 jalapeño, seeded and minced (optional)

1. Preheat oven to 350 degrees. Oil a 9 x 13-inch cake pan.
2. In small mixing bowl, whisk together flaxseed and water. Let stand for about 10 minutes to thicken.
3. In separate bowl, combine corn flour, cornmeal, sugar, baking powder, salt, and baking soda. Mix thoroughly.
4. In separate large bowl, combine soymilk, applesauce, oil, vinegar, and agave with the flaxseed mixture.
5. Using a rubber spatula, combine the wet mixture with the dry and mix well to thoroughly incorporate. Batter will be slightly runny. Fold in scallions and jalapeño.
6. Gently pour batter into prepared pan.
7. Bake 20–25 minutes, until edges are slightly golden brown.

THE STANFORD INN BY THE SEA FAMOUS SCONES

MAKES 16 SCONES

From the beginning, when we started serving continental breakfast in 1981, we wanted a truly special pastry. We thought of doing the baking ourselves and quickly realized that we did not have the space in our tiny kitchen; the kitchen sink was Alex and eventually Kate's bathtub. We went to local bakers and found the owner of a bakery with an old brick oven willing to create a spectacular coffee cake. Our guests enjoyed the products of his artistry for a number of years until he sold his business. Although he gave us the recipe, no one was able to duplicate what he had done.

We stumbled along without the coffee cake, and when we opened for breakfast at The Ravens, many of us got into the act of trying new pastry recipes, tasting many different versions of this classic. The result is a truly wonderful scone that has changed and been perfected over time.

---

9 tablespoons water

3 tablespoons Ener-G Egg Replacer (page 256)

2½ cups organic all-purpose flour

½ cup Sucanat or white sugar, plus more for sprinkling

4 teaspoons baking powder

½ teaspoon salt

¾ cup Earth Balance Vegan Shortening Sticks, chilled and cut into small cubes

½ cup soy creamer

Splash of vanilla extract

1 cup fresh or frozen berries or currants

2–3 tablespoons soymilk, soy creamer, or hemp milk

1. Preheat oven to 350 degrees.
2. In a food processor, whip the water and egg replacer for 1 minute. Set aside.
3. In a large bowl combine flour, Sucanat, baking powder, and salt. Cut in the Earth Balance cubes with a pastry cutter. (When you're finished, your mixture should look like small peas.)
4. Add egg replacer mixture to the flour mixture, along with the soy creamer and vanilla extract. With swift strokes, fold the wet mixture into the dry until the dough just comes together. Do not overmix.
5. Place mixture on a lightly floured surface and press together without overworking the dough. Flatten the dough with a rolling pin into a ½-inch-thick rectangle.
6. Push the fruit of your choice into half of the dough surface. Fold the dough in half once over the fruit and flatten again into 1-inch-thick rectangle.
7. Splash soymilk, creamer, or hemp milk on top, brushing evenly, then sprinkle with sugar.
8. Cut into 16 triangles and bake until golden brown, 30–40 minutes.

CLASSIC BREAKFAST MUFFINS

MAKES 8 MUFFINS

A breakfast treat, these muffins are like desserts—just one serving is fine, and not every day. Guests enjoy these and often ask for the recipe—it's another that causes people to say, "I can't believe there's no egg!"

2 cups all-purpose flour

1 cup sugar

1 teaspoon baking powder

1 teaspoon baking soda

½ teaspoon salt

1–2 tablespoons golden flaxseed, ground to fine powder

1 cup soymilk

½ cup water

⅓ cup coconut oil, melted

2 tablespoons organic applesauce

1 tablespoon lemon juice

1 teaspoon vanilla extract

¼ cup fruit (blueberries, chopped strawberries, bananas, etc.; optional)

1. Preheat oven to 350 degrees. Grease 8 cups of a muffin tin or line with muffin cups.
2. Whisk together flour, sugar, baking powder, baking soda, and salt in a large mixing bowl.
3. In a separate mixing bowl, whisk together flaxseed, soymilk, water, coconut oil, applesauce, lemon juice, and vanilla extract.
4. Add the wet mixture to the dry, and stir until just combined. Fold in fruit.
5. Spoon batter into the muffin tin, dividing among 8 muffin cups.
6. Bake for 15–20 minutes, until toothpick inserted into the middle of a muffin comes out clean.

SAUCES, DIPS & SPREADS

The recipes in this section often comprise the critical ingredients in our dishes. Their flavor profiles connect the various elements of a dish. The creamy Cashew Sauce (page 80), with its hint of sweetness, pulls together the slight bitterness and earthiness of braised greens with the citrus tang of the polenta in our signature dish, Citrus Polenta (page 46). On the other hand, dips and spreads help take the edge off hunger and provide a contrast to the chips, crostini, and crudité we serve as light appetizers.

BRAISING SAUCE

MAKES ABOUT 1 CUP

At The Ravens our basic braising sauce is called "tofu juice" because we once braised tofu in it. It was one of our first recipes, created to provide flavor for vegetables without sautéing. There is a small amount of sesame oil to enhance the flavors of garlic and ginger.

We have been using this sauce since the day we began serving cooked-to-order breakfasts to our guests. Keep it tightly sealed in your refrigerator and it should last a week.

---

1 tablespoon sesame oil
2 cloves garlic, finely chopped
Two ½-inch slices fresh ginger root
1 teaspoon turmeric
½ cup tamari
½ cup water

1. In a medium saucepan, heat the sesame oil, then add the garlic, ginger, and turmeric. Sauté for 1 minute, making sure the garlic does not burn.
2. Add the tamari and water, and simmer, uncovered, over medium heat for 15 minutes, stirring occasionally.
3. Refrigerate until ready to use.

KALE SAUCE

MAKES 2–3 CUPS

One of the three sauces used in our Indian-Spiced Polenta Napoleon (page 186), the Kale Sauce can also be warmed and used over vegetables or potatoes. We have used it with savory crepes, on bean patties, and with our Indian-Spiced Kale Potato Omelets (page 118).

Be careful when adding the jalapeño; heat varies from plant to plant. This sauce is whole-food goodness, and cooking class participants often request us to demonstrate it. There's no need: it is very simple.

---

1 bunch (about ½ pound) dinosaur kale

1 cup cashews, soaked for at least 20 minutes and drained

½ bunch (about 2 ounces) cilantro

½ jalapeño, seeded

1 teaspoon salt

Dash of cayenne pepper

2 cups water

Juice of 1 lemon

1. Steam kale for 3–4 minutes.
2. Combine steamed kale and remaining ingredients in a high-speed blender and process until smooth.
3. Let cool and store in the refrigerator for up to 3 days. Warm prior to serving.

CASHEW SAUCE

MAKES ABOUT 1½ CUPS

This delicately flavored sauce accompanies our Citrus Polenta with Braised Garden Greens and a Creamy Toasted Cashew Sauce (page 46), and can also be used over braised vegetables or as a mild gravy when thinned with additional soymilk. With the exception of soymilk, this sauce is dominated by whole foods.

2 cups raw cashews

2 tablespoons olive oil

½ red onion, finely chopped

1–2 shallots, finely chopped

2 tablespoons garlic, finely chopped

Small pinch of red pepper flakes

1 cup soymilk

Salt to taste

1. Preheat oven to 400 degrees.
2. Place cashews on a baking sheet and toast until golden, but not brown (about 4–5 minutes). Remove from the oven and cool.
3. Place cooled cashews in the bowl of a food processor fitted with a metal blade, and grind to a fine powder.
4. In a medium saucepan, heat the olive oil over medium heat, then add onion and shallots and simmer until soft. Add garlic and red pepper flakes. Turn down the heat to medium-low and allow the mixture to caramelize, until the onions and shallots are soft and light brown.
5. Transfer cashews and onion mixture to a high-speed blender. Puree while slowly adding the soymilk.
6. Blend until smooth and creamy, then add salt to taste.
7. Store in the refrigerator for up to 3 days. This sauce is easily reheated.

CASHEW BÉCHAMEL

MAKES 1 CUP

Sauces were used historically to cover the tastes of spoiled meats. Béchamel is a mild sauce that serves not to obscure flavors, but to join them. Acting as an officiant, the sauce marries the flavors of the more substantive vegetable layers in hot dishes such as our Moussaka (page 233), or chilled dishes like our Salad Napoleon (page 142).

1 cup raw cashews, soaked and drained

1 shallot, roughly chopped

1 tablespoon nutritional yeast

1 tablespoon minced fresh thyme or 1 teaspoon dried thyme

2 cloves garlic

1 teaspoon salt

½ cup water

Juice and zest of 1 lemon

2 tablespoons olive oil

1 tablespoon white balsamic vinegar or white wine vinegar

1. Combine all ingredients in high-speed blender and puree until completely smooth.
2. Periodically, stop machine and scrape down sides to help incorporate mixture.
3. Season with additional salt and lemon juice to taste.

HOLLANDAISE SAUCE

MAKES 1½ CUPS

We regularly hear, "I can't believe there's no egg!" when we serve our Hollandaise Sauce. Traditional Hollandaise is simply a yellow mélange with lemon, egg yolk, fat, and a hint of spice. In our sauce, turmeric provides the color, tofu replaces the egg, and olive oil and Earth Balance provide the fat. A simple recipe, the sauce should be served fresh rather than stored and reheated.

6 ounces silken tofu

¼ teaspoon turmeric

Salt and pepper to taste

2 tablespoons olive oil

1–2 tablespoons lemon juice to taste

Dash of habanero sauce

½ cup Earth Balance Original Buttery Spread or similar, melted

1. Using high-speed blender, puree all ingredients, except the Earth Balance, until smooth.
2. Keeping the blender running, slowly stream in the Earth Balance. Blend until the mixture is well incorporated and emulsified.

SEE PHOTO ON PAGE 75

RAVENS LEMON TAHINI SAUCE

MAKES 1½ CUPS

This sauce was inspired by our desire to provide a more savory alternative to the buttery flavor of our Hollandaise Sauce (page 81). Tahini lends an earthiness, complementing greens and fungi, while the lemon adds a contrasting hint of acid.

This sauce holds better than our Hollandaise and can be reheated.

---

8 ounces silken tofu

½ teaspoon salt, plus more to taste

¼ teaspoon turmeric (add more for a deeper yellow color)

Small pinch of cayenne pepper

¼ cup plus ½ tablespoon lemon juice

¼ cup tahini

¼ cup soymilk

Dash of habanero sauce

Salt to taste

1. Place tofu in a saucepan and cover with water. Over high heat, boil the tofu for 5 minutes. Drain off all water.
2. Place the tofu in a food processor with the remaining ingredients. Blend until smooth and creamy. Add salt to taste.
3. Serve immediately or store in the refrigerator and reheat.

TOFU RAITA

Raita is traditionally a yogurt-based condiment. This version uses tofu and remains as light and refreshing as the original, without the dairy. We use Tofu Raita for multiple purposes, including in different amuse-bouches—filling a roasted cremini mushroom cap, atop flaxseed crackers or crostini, in a celery crevice, or with baby lettuce.

16 ounces medium-firm tofu (not silken)

1 tablespoon ground coriander

½ tablespoon ground cumin

¼ teaspoon cayenne pepper

½ tablespoon salt

¼ cup lemon juice (from 2–3 lemons)

2 tablespoons apple cider vinegar

1 English cucumber, peeled and diced

½ cup diced red onion

½ bunch (about ½ ounce) mint, stemmed and chopped roughly

1. Combine tofu, coriander, cumin, cayenne pepper, salt, lemon juice, and vinegar in food processor and process until incorporated.
2. Transfer tofu mixture to a bowl and add cucumber, onion, and mint, and mix thoroughly. Season with additional salt and lemon juice if desired.
3. If mixture is watery, place it in a clean dish towel (or cheesecloth), and strain excess liquid.
4. Store sealed in the refrigerator for up to 3 days.

CILANTRO MINT PESTO

MAKES 1 CUP

If you planted mint in your garden, you probably have more mint than you know what to do with and are tasked with pulling it out. We find that we don't need too much for mojitos and the very rarely ordered mint julep. This sauce is a great way to burn through this *Lamiaceae*—Latin for mint or deadnettle family, which includes chia, nettle, and oregano.

Used in our Indian-Spiced Polenta Napoleon (page 186), it is also a versatile pesto that adds zest to steamed or grilled vegetables; is great as a condiment in sandwiches; and can be used in amuse-bouche, as with our Tofu Raita (page 83).

1½ cups tightly packed cilantro (stems may be included)

1½ cups tightly packed mint

2 tablespoons coconut flakes, toasted

1 jalapeño pepper, seeded

½ teaspoon salt

1½ tablespoons red wine vinegar

2 tablespoons olive oil, or more if needed

1. Combine all ingredients except oil in a food processor.
2. With the food processor running, slowly stream in oil until a smooth paste is achieved. Scrape down sides several times if necessary.
3. Store in the refrigerator for up to a week.

CASHEW MOREL CREAM

MAKES 1½ CUPS

This is a deeply satisfying sauce made with the magnificent morel. These mushrooms are usually harvested in the spring and are most often found in markets in dried form.

½ cup dried morels, rehydrated in 1 cup water for 30 minutes (reserve soaking liquid)

½ cup cashews, soaked overnight and drained

1 shallot, roughly chopped

1 tablespoon fresh thyme

½ teaspoon salt

Juice of ½ lemon

1 tablespoon white balsamic vinegar

1 tablespoon olive oil

Water as needed

1. Combine all ingredients, except for the morel soaking liquid and water, in a high-speed blender. Puree until all ingredients are well incorporated.
2. With the blender running, stream in morel soaking liquid to fully incorporate mixture. If a creamier consistency is desired, add extra water.
3. Store in the refrigerator for up to a week.

SALSA CRUDA

MAKES ABOUT 3½ CUPS

This fresh vegetable salsa is a particular staff favorite. We serve it on tofu, our house potatoes, tempeh, bread, polenta, and sometimes just wrapped into a corn tortilla. It's so good it can stand on its own! By the way, some chefs call this recipe salsa fresca or pico de gallo, which means "beak of a rooster."

3 pounds Roma or saladette tomatoes, diced

1 medium red onion, diced small

¾ bunch (about 3 ounces) cilantro, chopped

½ jalapeño pepper, seeded and diced

1 tablespoon salt

Juice of 2 limes

1. Combine all ingredients in a large mixing bowl and mix together.
2. Store in an airtight container in the refrigerator until ready to use.

PUMPKIN SEED, ARUGULA, AND MINT PESTO

MAKES ¾–1 CUP

This pesto combines all the nutritional benefits of pumpkin seeds, arugula, and mint in a flavorful condiment. It is bursting with flavor from the pepperiness of arugula to the clean crispness of mint. We use this pesto as an amuse-bouche, putting it on crackers, filling a small roasted cremini mushroom cap, and layering between a cucumber slice and half a cherry tomato.

1 cup baby arugula
½ cup fresh mint leaves
¼ cup shelled pumpkin seeds, soaked in hot water for 30 minutes and drained
1 bunch (about 4 ounces) basil
1 clove garlic
½ teaspoon salt
½ teaspoon pepper
¼ cup olive oil

1. In food processor, combine all ingredients except oil. Process until well incorporated.
2. With the processor running, drizzle the olive oil into the mixture in a steady stream, until a paste texture is achieved.

WASABI SAUCE

MAKES ABOUT ½ CUP

This sauce's popularity gave rise to efforts to grow wasabi at the inn. It is an expensive condiment—so much so that most of what passes for wasabi in the market is actually horseradish. True wasabi is not harsh and has a greater complexity than horseradish. We use this sauce to accent the sweetness of our Tamari-Maple Glazed Tofu (page 123). It can also serve to replace mustard on burgers.

2¼ tablespoons wasabi powder

2¼ tablespoons water

2¼ tablespoons canola oil

1½ teaspoons agave syrup

1. In a small bowl, make a paste of the wasabi and water.
2. Place paste, oil, and agave into a food processor fitted with a metal blade. Process until smooth and creamy. Add more water if necessary.
3. Refrigerate for up to a week.

MARINARA SAUCE

MAKES ABOUT 1 CUP

We use this versatile sauce on pizza, children's pasta, and our Eggplant Cannelloni (page 192). It is our base Italian sauce that can be spiced with the addition of chili pepper, or made tangier with the addition of pickled capers.

½ cup diced onion
(yellow or red)

1 tablespoon olive oil

1 tablespoon minced garlic

1 tablespoon chiffonade
fresh basil

1 teaspoon dried basil

1 teaspoon dried oregano

1 teaspoon dried parsley

1 teaspoon salt

⅛ teaspoon ground
black pepper

4 cups diced fresh tomatoes
(reserve liquid and seeds)

1. In a medium saucepan, sauté the onion in the olive oil over medium heat to soften, about 3 minutes.

2. Add the garlic and sauté an additional 1–2 minutes, or until fragrant but not browned, stirring constantly.

3. Add the fresh basil, the dried herbs, salt, and pepper, and sauté an additional 30 seconds.

4. Add the tomatoes and reserved liquid and seeds. Stir well to combine. Reduce the heat to low, and simmer the mixture for 10 minutes to blend the flavors.

5. Blend to smooth the sauce, or serve chunky if preferred.

BALSAMIC REDUCTION

MAKES ¼ CUP

This is a great recipe that can add style and design, as well as flavor, to any dish. When it is refrigerated, the Balsamic Reduction can last for up to three months. Reheat to room temperature before using for best results.

1 cup balsamic vinegar

1. Place vinegar in a saucepan and simmer until liquid is reduced to ¼ cup, about 1½ hours.
2. Cool and place in a squeeze bottle in order to produce a design over the food, such as a squiggle. This sauce can also be drizzled from a spoon. Serve at room temperature.

RAVENS BARBECUE SAUCE

MAKES ABOUT 3 CUPS

This sauce is inspired by the great barbecue for which Kansas City and the Ozarks are known. Jeff grew up in that region learning how to slow smoke meat (which provides barbecue's true flavor base). Barbecue sauce balances the pungency of the smoke. This recipe provides both smokiness and sweetness, and we serve it with smoked portobellos, grilled braised tempeh or tofu, and bean-based burgers. If you are seeking a greater smokiness, use smoked chipotle powder.

1 large yellow onion, diced (about 2 cups)

¼ cup minced garlic

2 tablespoons olive oil

3 cups tomato paste

2 tablespoons paprika

2 tablespoons chili powder

1 teaspoon chipotle flakes or powder

2 cups apple cider vinegar

2 cups water

1 cup vegan Worcestershire sauce

2½ cups maple syrup

Salt to taste

1. Sauté the onion and garlic in olive oil over medium heat until the onions are translucent.
2. Add tomato paste, paprika, chili powder, and chipotle flakes, and cook for about 10 minutes to enhance the flavors.
3. Add apple cider vinegar, water, and Worcestershire sauce, and cook for about 30 minutes over medium-low heat.
4. Remove from heat and strain through a chinois. Place strained mixture back into the saucepan and add the maple syrup. Allow sauce to thicken for approximately 20–25 minutes over low heat. Season with salt.
5. Remove sauce from heat and serve warm.
6. Store in the refrigerator for up to a week.

WHITE BEAN HUMMUS

MAKES ABOUT 2½ CUPS

This great hummus is often requested by brides-to-be and served with crudité for their wedding receptions. Our recipe is very light on oil as there's no need for the oil wash found in chickpea-based hummus.

FOR THE ROASTED GARLIC

2–3 bulbs garlic

Olive oil

Salt

FOR THE HUMMUS AND ASSEMBLY

3 cups cooked white beans (reserve liquid)

¼ cup tahini

Salt and black pepper to taste

⅓–½ cup Ravens All-Purpose Vegetable Stock (page 163) or store-bought vegan broth

¼ cup olive oil

3 tablespoons lemon juice

2–3 tablespoons chopped fresh rosemary

For the Roasted Garlic

1. Preheat oven to 425 degrees.
2. Cut the bottoms and tops off the garlic bulbs.
3. Place the bulbs on a sheet of aluminum foil, drizzle with olive oil, sprinkle with salt, and wrap tightly in the foil.
4. Bake for about 30 minutes, until nice and golden on top. The cloves of garlic should yield easily to pressure. Cool.

For the Hummus and Assembly

1. In a food processor, combine the white beans, tahini, salt and pepper, cooking liquid, olive oil, and lemon juice.
2. Squeeze out each individual clove of roasted garlic and add to the food processor.
3. Blend well, and adjust seasonings to taste (add more salt and pepper, or lemon juice as necessary).
4. Sprinkle rosemary on top and serve.

TOMATO CHUTNEY

MAKES 1 CUP

This tasty chutney goes well with any eastern Indian dish. Dip naan into it, serve it with grilled vegetables, or dollop on vegan burgers.

1 pound fresh tomatoes, diced (Romas are a good choice)

Pinch of salt

1 teaspoon brown mustard seeds

1 teaspoon fennel seeds

1 teaspoon cumin seeds

1 teaspoon coriander seeds

1 teaspoon red pepper flakes

1 small yellow onion, diced

1 teaspoon grated fresh ginger

½ red bell pepper, diced

1 tablespoon sunflower oil

1 cup sugar

¼ cup tamarind paste

½ cup brown rice vinegar

¼ cup apple cider vinegar

1. Bring tomatoes and salt to a simmer in a saucepan on the stove, and reduce juices for 30–35 minutes.

2. In a sauté pan, dry toast the mustard seeds, fennel seeds, cumin seeds, coriander seeds, and red pepper flakes. Add the onion, ginger, red bell pepper, and sunflower oil and stir to combine.

3. Add the sugar, tamarind paste, and vinegars, and simmer for 10 minutes.

4. Add reduced tomatoes to the tamarind paste mixture. Season with salt and/or sugar to taste.

5. Store in airtight container for 7 days or longer.

MUSHROOM WALNUT PÂTÉ

MAKES ¾ CUP

All of our pâtés are popular, but the Mushroom Walnut Pâté is the most preferred
by our staff. The reason why: we always stock the ingredients and it is easy
and quick to make. Serve this in mixed company—vegans and carnivores. It's
guaranteed to impress both.

---

1 portobello mushroom
1 shiitake mushroom
Spray oil or 1 tablespoon olive oil
½ cup walnuts, toasted
2 cloves garlic
Fresh thyme (optional)
Juice of ½ lemon

1. Slice mushrooms.
2. Lightly coat the bottom of a small sauté pan with oil and heat over medium heat.
3. Add mushroom and sauté until soft and slightly browned, about 5 minutes.
4. Add the sautéed mushrooms and remaining ingredients to a food processor and blend until smooth.
5. Let the sauce cool.

CHIPOTLE SAUCE

MAKES ABOUT 3 CUPS

With its tomatoes and chipotle pepper, this salsa gives a slightly smoky, tangy flavor to our Stanford Ranchero and Santa Fe Burrito (page 54).

---

1 tablespoon olive oil

1 small yellow onion, diced

½ tablespoon chopped garlic

2 teaspoons finely ground dried chipotle peppers

1 tablespoon dried oregano

½ tablespoon sugar

1 teaspoon black pepper

1 (14.5-ounce) can organic diced tomatoes

½ tablespoon salt

¾ cup water

1. In a medium stockpot, heat the olive oil over medium heat, add the onion, and sauté until translucent, then add the garlic, sautéing for 2–3 additional minutes.
2. Add the chipotle peppers, oregano, sugar, and pepper. Combine well and continue to sauté another 2 minutes.
3. Add tomatoes, salt, and water. Simmer over medium-low heat for 20 minutes.
4. Lightly blend the mixture with a hand mixer or in a blender. Add more salt to taste.

RAVENS ENCHILADA SAUCE

This sauce is used in our chilaquiles recipe (page 58). Unlike other enchilada sauces, ours uses very little oil. The chipotle provides a distinctive flavor.

½ cup diced red onion
1 teaspoon minced garlic
1 teaspoon sunflower oil
1 tablespoon salt
½ tablespoon chili powder
½ tablespoon ground cumin
1 teaspoon chipotle powder
½ teaspoon black pepper
¼ cup chopped cilantro
½ cup tomato paste
2½ cups tomato juice
½ cup water
1 tablespoon lime juice

1. In a skillet over medium heat, sauté onion and garlic in oil until soft. Add salt and spices and cook for 1 more minute.
2. Add cilantro, tomato paste, and tomato juice and cook for 15 minutes.
3. Add water and lime juice and blend well with an immersion blender or in a high-speed blender.
4. Store in the refrigerator for up to a week.

REMOULADE

MAKES 2 CUPS

When Jeff was growing up, his mom made remoulade with mayonnaise, Dijon mustard, chives, and chopped hard-boiled eggs. He loved it on everything from fish sticks to sandwiches with leftover turkey. This remoulade is substantially different, but still provides a tangy flavor to counter the oils/fats in other foods. We serve this with our Crab-less Cakes (page 129) in crab cake competitions.

12.3 ounces silken tofu

Juice and zest of 1 lime

1 tablespoon white wine vinegar

1 teaspoon Dijon mustard

1 tablespoon nutritional yeast

1 teaspoon salt

¼ teaspoon pepper

1 scallion, white and light green parts, chopped

¼ cup capers

1. In a medium bowl, whisk together tofu, lime juice and zest, white wine vinegar, and Dijon mustard.
2. Add nutritional yeast, salt, and pepper, and whisk until combined.
3. Add scallion and capers. Whisk until evenly distributed.
4. Refrigerate until ready to use. Serve cold.

CARROT PÂTÉ

MAKES 1½ CUPS

This recipe has great flavor and is perfect for a special reception. Serve as a dip or spread with crudité or crostini.

1½ cups cashew pieces

1 cup peeled and roughly chopped carrot

2 tablespoons tahini

2 tablespoons red or white mellow miso

1 tablespoon gluten-free tamari

1–2 tablespoons water

Salt and pepper to taste

1. Place all ingredients except salt and pepper in a high-speed blender and blend, starting with 1 tablespoon of water. Add an additional tablespoon of water if the mixture is too thick to easily spread.
2. With a rubber spatula, carefully scrape sides of the blender and continue to blend until a smooth paste is formed. Add salt and pepper to taste.
3. Store in the refrigerator until ready to use.

CLASSIC CHICKPEA HUMMUS

MAKES 3½ CUPS

Here's a classic hummus based on the chickpea. We always cook the beans with a strip of kombu, a seaweed that tenderizes the chickpeas, making them more digestible. To add extra flavor interest to our brand of hummus, we toast cumin seeds and grind them ourselves. The toasting intensifies the cumin and adds a touch of smokiness. If you don't have cumin seeds, ground cumin will serve.

1¼ cups chickpeas, soaked in 4 cups water overnight in the refrigerator and drained

3–4 cloves garlic

1 strip dried kombu (optional)

6 cups water

¼ cup tahini

2 teaspoons cumin seeds, toasted and ground (see note)

Juice of 2 lemons

1 tablespoon olive oil

½ teaspoon habanero sauce (optional)

Salt and pepper to taste

Chopped parsley or chives (optional)

1. Place chickpeas, garlic, kombu, and water in a large pot. Cover and simmer over medium heat until tender, about 25–30 minutes. Let cool and pick out kombu strip.
2. Drain beans and garlic, reserving the liquid.
3. Place beans, garlic, tahini, cumin, lemon juice, olive oil, and habanero sauce in food processor. Process while drizzling in 1–2 cups of the reserved cooking liquid, until a thick paste forms.
4. Add salt and pepper to taste. Fold in chopped parsley or chives. Serve warm or chilled.

   Cumin Note: To toast the seeds, place in a sauté pan over moderate heat until the seeds turn darker and begin to pop. Remove from heat and grind in a spice grinder or dedicated coffee grinder.

KALAMATA OLIVE PÂTÉ

MAKES 2 CUPS

A favorite recipe at the inn, this pâté is easy to make, but not necessarily inexpensive. Use quality Kalamatas.

1 bunch (about 4 ounces) parsley

4 cloves garlic

3 (12-ounce) jars pitted Kalamata olives

Zest of 1 lemon

Juice of 2 lemons

1 tablespoon olive oil

1. In a food processor, process parsley and garlic until minced.
2. Add olives, lemon zest, and lemon juice and continue to process.
3. With the food processor running, drizzle in the olive oil to create a creamy texture.
4. Serve immediately or store in the refrigerator.

APPETIZERS & SIDES

On The Ravens' menu, appetizers and sides are "small plates." We bring the same attention to them that we do to our entrées. A salad and a side can be a full meal. The dishes that follow help make our menu more flavorful and interesting, and nearly every dish has been an entrée before we reduced the size of the portions.

BLACK-EYED PEA CAKES

4-6 SERVINGS, OR 10-12 CAKES

A New Year's celebratory dish! In the American Southeast, black-eyed peas are eaten on New Year's Day to ensure prosperity. Our Black-Eyed Pea Cakes are our nod to this tradition. These patties are crispy and delicious and can be served on their own, on braised greens (the color of money), or as burger sliders.

There's no better way to start a New Year than with a whole-food, plant-based, ethically sourced dish. Our cakes are healthy for you and the planet.

FOR THE BLACK-EYED PEA CAKES

2–3 cups black-eyed peas
1 bay leaf
1 strip dried kombu
2 tablespoons olive oil
½ cup minced red onion
½ cup minced red bell pepper
½ cup minced celery
½ cup minced potato
4 cloves minced garlic

1 jalapeño, seeded and minced
1 tablespoon nutritional yeast
2 teaspoons salt
1 teaspoon ground cumin
1 teaspoon paprika
1 teaspoon chili powder
¼ teaspoon black pepper
⅛ teaspoon cayenne pepper
1 cup gluten-free oats
1 tablespoon marinara sauce or tomato paste

2 tablespoons ground flaxseeds
¼ cup chopped scallion
2 tablespoons chopped cilantro
2 tablespoons sunflower oil

FOR THE CHIPOTLE DIPPING SAUCE

¼–½ teaspoon chipotle powder
Pinch of salt
¼ cup Tangy Sour Crème (page 262)
½ teaspoon lime juice

For the Black-Eyed Pea Cakes

1. In a large saucepan, cover black-eyed peas with at least 2 inches water. Add bay leaf and kombu and bring to a boil, then lower heat and simmer for 60 minutes, or until beans are tender. Remove from heat and cool. Set aside ½ cup whole peas.
2. Place olive oil, onion, pepper, celery, potato, garlic, and jalapeño in large sauté pan and sauté over medium heat until the vegetables are coated with the oil. Add nutritional yeast and spices and continue sautéing until vegetables are soft. Let mixture cool.
3. Pulse oats in food processor until ground; set aside in a bowl.
4. Add the black-eyed peas to the food processor and pulse, leaving some chunks. Set aside.
5. In a large bowl, combine the sautéed vegetable mixture, ½ cup of pulsed oats, marinara sauce, 1 cup of pulsed peas, the reserved ½ cup whole peas, and ground flaxseeds. Mix together thoroughly.

Recipe continued on next page . . .

6. Add more peas or oats to reach desired consistency (not too moist, and not too dry). Then fold in the scallion and chopped cilantro.

7. Cover bowl, and let set in fridge for 20 minutes or overnight.

8. Preheat oven to 300 degrees. Coat a baking sheet with the sunflower oil.

9. Form cakes using a ⅓-cup dry measuring cup or small ice cream scooper.

10. Bake for 15 minutes. Flip cakes, then bake 10 more minutes, or until a crust has formed on both sides. (If freezing, shorten baking time by 10 minutes total.)

11. Serve with Chipotle Dipping Sauce.

For the Chipotle Dipping Sauce

1. Combine all ingredients in a mixing bowl, stir well, and serve.

LIME-INFUSED ROASTED ASPARAGUS WITH MOREL SAUCE

4-6 SERVINGS

Asparagus and morels are harbingers of spring—asparagus in gardens and farms and morels in forests, particularly those recovering from fire. Because roasting asparagus enhances its flavor, we often forgo the extra ingredients and just lightly spray the asparagus and grill it, turning frequently, until the asparagus becomes a rich green.

1½ pounds asparagus (about 1 bunch), cleaned and 1 inch trimmed off bottom

1 teaspoon garlic powder (optional)

½ teaspoon salt

1 tablespoon olive oil

Zest of 1 lime

¼ cup Cashew Morel Cream (page 86)

1. Preheat oven to 350 degrees.
2. Combine asparagus, garlic powder, salt, and oil on sheet tray and toss together, making sure asparagus spears are evenly coated.
3. Roast for 15 minutes, until asparagus is tender and golden brown, shaking pan halfway through cooking time to ensure asparagus is evenly cooked.
4. Serve hot or chilled, garnished with lime zest sprinkled evenly over asparagus. Serve Cashew Morel Cream drizzled over the asparagus spears or on the side.

TRUMPET ROYALE OR TOFU SATAY WITH PEANUT SAUCE

4-6 SERVINGS

This is a wonderful dish that can be served as an appetizer or an entrée. You can substitute tofu for the trumpet royale mushrooms. When making the peanut sauce, be sure to carefully add the chili paste to ensure you are within your personal heat tolerance. We often serve this dish as an appetizer with the Asian Sesame Slaw (page 160). Note: As an appetizer allow two mushrooms per serving, which, depending on size, will make 4-6 separate skewered slices. When using tofu, allow 3 skewered slices per serving.

FOR THE TRUMPET ROYALE OR TOFU SATAY

12 king trumpet mushrooms or 1 (16-ounce) block firm tofu (if using tofu, omit the olive oil below)

½ cup tamari

½ cup maple syrup

¼ cup olive oil

1½ teaspoons minced garlic

1½ teaspoons minced ginger

FOR THE PEANUT SAUCE

1 tablespoon sunflower oil

½ cup sliced red onion

1½ teaspoons minced ginger

1½ teaspoons minced garlic

2 teaspoons Thai Kitchen red chili paste

¼ cup chopped cilantro

3 tablespoons brown sugar

1 tablespoon granulated sugar

Salt to taste

¼ cup rice vinegar

Juice of 1 lime

1 tablespoon gluten-free tamari

½ cup coconut milk

¾ cup creamy peanut butter

For the Trumpet Royale or Tofu Satay

1. Slice the trumpets lengthwise, approximately ¼ inch thick. If using tofu, cut the tofu lengthwise into 4 even slices.
2. Marinate for an hour in the remaining ingredients.
3. Skewer each mushroom or tofu slice.
4. Grill or griddle the mushrooms or tofu slices until grill marks show, or they're slightly browned. Remove from heat.
5. Serve with Peanut Sauce.

For the Peanut Sauce

1. Heat the oil in a large skillet over medium heat.
2. Add the onion and ginger; cook, stirring frequently, until browned.
3. Add the garlic and chili paste, and brown lightly.
4. Add the cilantro, sugars, salt, rice vinegar, lime juice, and tamari.
5. Bring the mixture to a boil, add the coconut milk, and return to a boil.
6. Transfer mixture to a blender or food processor and puree.
7. Return to the skillet and bring to a simmer.
8. Slowly whisk in the peanut butter until melted and combined.
9. Serve on the side with the grilled trumpets or tofu.

CAULIFLOWER CEVICHE

MAKES 6–7 CUPS

This flavorful dish can be served as a dip, as a salad on a bed of cabbage or lettuce, or on its own in a small martini glass as an appetizer.

We served a vegan ceviche for years, using marinated turnip to represent scallops in traditional seafood ceviche. Turnips, although a brassica, are reminiscent of a mild radish and do not fit well with the other elements of the ceviche.

One of our cooks, who began as a dishwasher and became a line cook, re-created the dish using cauliflower, vastly improving the flavor profile. Chilled cauliflower is sweet without the sulfur accents and does not taste like a radish. By the way, this dish can be entirely raw.

About 3 cups cauliflower florets (from 1 large head or 2 small heads cauliflower)

5 tomatoes, diced small

1 red onion, diced small

1 bunch (about 4 ounces) cilantro, chopped

1 jalapeño, seeded and minced

2 teaspoons salt

1 teaspoon black pepper (optional)

Juice of 2 limes

1. Steam or boil the cauliflower florets until soft. Cool and cut into small chunks. If making a raw version of this recipe, break the florets apart but don't cook them.
2. Mix all ingredients in a large bowl and chill. Add more salt and jalapeño if desired.

   To make a raw version: Mix all ingredients except tomatoes in a large bowl, cover, and refrigerate overnight, turning the mixture occasionally. Before serving, add the tomatoes and toss.

DOLMAS

MAKES ABOUT 12 DOLMAS

A great finger food, dolmas are best made with grape leaves because they are tender. In Northern California, we have difficulty finding organic grape leaves, so we substitute lacinato kale, otherwise known as dinosaur kale. The leaves are large and can be tenderized. Use the youngest leaves.

---

12 lacinato kale leaves

3 cups cool water

1 tablespoon white vinegar

1 tablespoon salt

2 tablespoons olive oil, divided

1 large white onion, diced

¼ cup minced garlic

1½ cups brown rice

1 cup roughly chopped almonds

Zest of 1 lemon

3 cups Ravens All-Purpose Vegetable Stock (page 163) or store-bought vegan broth

½ cup lemon juice

½ cup minced parsley

3 tablespoons chopped dill

1. To create malleable kale for rolling, first, blanch kale: Place leaves in a large sauté pan, cover with boiling water, and let sit for 3–5 minutes. Drain.

2. Place the kale in pan with the 3 cups cool water, vinegar, and salt and soak leaves for at least 2 hours.

3. In a large sauté pan, sauté 1 tablespoon of the olive oil, onion, and garlic over medium heat. Add brown rice, almonds, lemon zest, vegetable stock, and lemon juice. Cook until rice is partially cooked (not hard, but not done).

4. Cool mixture, and add parsley and dill.

5. Preheat oven to 350 degrees.

6. To assemble, place approximately 1 teaspoon of the rice mixture in center of a kale leaf, fold in leaf ends, and roll.

7. Put rolled dolmas in a baking dish, add the remaining 1 tablespoon olive oil, and bake for 40 minutes.

INDIAN-SPICED KALE AND POTATO OMELET

6 SERVINGS

This dish is inspired by the traditional Spanish tortilla, which is an omelet of eggs, chunks of potatoes, and onion that is almost always served at room temperature. We created a robust version by adapting our chickpea crepe and filling it with kale, potatoes, and East Indian spices. This is a versatile appetizer that seems more like savory pancakes than omelets.

Asked to bring a unique appetizer to Taste of Mendocino's showcase of Mendocino wines in San Francisco, we contributed this dish. We also brought a redwood outrigger canoe and a hand-built, lightweight suspended mountain bike to demonstrate the variety and vitality of Mendocino recreational activities. Attendees were interested in the bike and outrigger canoe—and they were stoked to have something other than bread or high-calorie, high-fat appetizers served at the venue. Attendees simply circled, politely taking one at a time, many times over.

FOR THE BATTER

12.3 ounces silken tofu
2 cloves garlic
2 tablespoons nutritional yeast
1 teaspoon salt
½ teaspoon turmeric
½ cup chickpea flour
1 tablespoon arrowroot powder or cornstarch

FOR THE FILLING

1 tablespoon olive oil
1 medium onion, diced small
¼ cup diced red bell pepper
1 clove garlic, minced
1 cup chopped kale
½ cup boiled, peeled, and diced potato
1 teaspoon ground cumin
1 teaspoon chili powder
1 teaspoon paprika
Juice of 1 lime
½ teaspoon turmeric
Salt and pepper to taste

For the Batter

1. Preheat oven to 350 degrees.
2. Combine the tofu, garlic, nutritional yeast, salt, and turmeric in a high-speed blender, blending until smooth.
3. Add the chickpea flour and arrowroot powder to the blender and puree the mixture another 10 seconds to fully incorporate. Set mixture aside.

For the Filling

1. In an oven-safe sauté pan, combine the oil, onion, bell pepper, and garlic. Sauté over medium heat for 5 minutes or until vegetables are soft.
2. Add the kale and potato and cook approximately 3 minutes, or until kale is wilted.
3. Add the remaining ingredients and cook for 3–5 minutes, to fully coat the vegetables.
4. Once all is incorporated, pour batter over the vegetable mixture and cook over low heat for 5 minutes.
5. Remove the pan from the stove and bake in the oven for another 10 minutes, or until the top is golden brown.
6. Remove from oven and let cool slightly before serving.

Note: You can simplify the recipe by using curry powder instead of cumin, chili powder, paprika and turmeric in the filling. Serve with Tofu Raita (page 83).

AFRICAN ROLLS WITH SWEET POTATO COULIS

4-6 SERVINGS

Bright collard greens make these African Rolls stand out. Depending on the number you offer, these rolls can serve as a salad, an appetizer, or an entrée. Because you can prepare them ahead of time, you can hang out with your guests rather than cook.

We serve these as a New Year's special: the collard greens suggest money and the black-eyed peas prosperity.

FOR THE COLLARD GREENS

1 bunch (about ½ pound) collard greens, cleaned and stemmed

3 tablespoons tamari

2 tablespoons olive oil

FOR THE BLACK-EYED PEAS

1 cup dried black-eyed peas

1 teaspoon salt

4 cups water

FOR THE OKRA AND AFRICAN ROLL ASSEMBLY

2 tablespoons olive oil

½ cup onion

2 teaspoons minced ginger

2 teaspoons minced garlic

1 jalapeño pepper, seeded and minced

½ teaspoon salt

3 cups ½-inch-thick sliced okra

2 teaspoons ground coriander

2 teaspoons ground cinnamon

1 teaspoon paprika

½ teaspoon freshly ground black pepper

½ teaspoon allspice

¼ teaspoon cayenne

Pinch of nutmeg

½ cup water

Juice of ½ lemon

FOR THE SWEET POTATO COULIS

1 tablespoon oil

½ cup diced onion

1 tablespoon minced ginger

1 tablespoon ground coriander

1 tablespoon paprika

1 teaspoon ground cumin

1 teaspoon ground cinnamon

1 teaspoon garlic powder

½ teaspoon red pepper flakes

½ cup water

2 cups peeled and diced sweet potato

1½ teaspoons salt

¼ teaspoon pepper

Juice of 1 orange

1 tablespoon agave syrup (optional)

For the Collard Greens

1. Toss collard leaves with tamari and olive oil in a large bowl. Let marinate for 30–60 minutes.
2. Set aside.

Recipe continued on next page . . .

For the Black-Eyed Peas

1. In medium saucepan, combine all ingredients. Bring to a boil, reduce heat, and cook until black-eyed peas are tender, approximately 30–60 minutes.
2. Drain and set aside.

For the Okra and African Roll Assembly

1. In sauté pan, combine olive oil, onion, ginger, garlic, jalapeño pepper, and salt over low heat. Cook until onions are translucent and vegetables are tender, about 10 minutes.
2. Raise heat to medium. Add okra, coriander, cinnamon, paprika, black pepper, allspice, cayenne, nutmeg, and water. Simmer until okra is tender and liquid is absorbed, approximately 15 minutes.
3. Add lemon juice and mix well. Remove from heat and set aside to cool.
4. Transfer to large mixing bowl and fold in the black-eyed peas. Season with additional salt and pepper to taste.
5. Lay marinated collard green leaf, shiny side down, on cutting board or clean surface. If leaf is cut in half lengthwise due to stemming, overlap two sides to form a complete sheet.
6. Place about ¼ cup of filling on the bottom of each leaf (leaving about ½ inch exposed leaf underneath). Roll leaf over once to cover filling. Fold both sides inward to seal everything in. Carefully start rolling from the bottom up until roll is formed. Repeat until all leaves are filled.
7. Serve rolls chilled or steamed. If steaming, cook for about 10 minutes, or until heated thoroughly. Serve with the Sweet Potato Coulis.

For the Sweet Potato Coulis

1. In sauté pan, heat olive oil, onion, and ginger over medium-low heat until onions are translucent, about 5 minutes.
2. Add coriander, paprika, cumin, cinnamon, garlic, and red pepper flakes. Cook for 1–2 minutes to toast the spices. Add the water to deglaze the pan.
3. Add sweet potatoes to the onion mixture. Raise heat to medium and cook mixture for about 10–15 minutes, or until sweet potatoes are tender and water is absorbed.
4. Let mixture cool slightly.
5. Transfer to food processor and add remaining ingredients. Process until mixture is smooth and creamy. Scrape down sides of food processor bowl as necessary to ensure the mixture is well combined.
6. Season with additional salt, pepper, or agave to taste.

TAMARI-MAPLE-GLAZED TOFU

MAKES 9 TOFU LOGS

We serve sticks of Tamari-Maple-Glazed Tofu with our Wasabi Sauce (page 90).
The tangy sauce is a tasty contrast to the sweetness of the glaze. To set the glaze,
we grill the tofu. This glazed tofu is great on top of any salad or bed of greens.

16 ounces extra-firm tofu

1 teaspoon garlic powder or 2
cloves garlic, chopped

1 teaspoon grated ginger

1 cup maple syrup

¼ cup tamari

Salt to taste

Spray oil

Wasabi Sauce, for serving
(page 90)

1. Cut tofu into ¾-inch logs by cutting three slabs from one side of
   tofu block and then cutting the three slabs into logs for a total of
   nine logs.

2. In a mixing bowl, combine the garlic, ginger, maple syrup, and
   tamari and mix thoroughly.

3. Dust tofu logs with salt and spray with oil.

4. Broil or griddle tofu logs until golden.

5. Remove tofu from heat and place in a sauté pan along with sauce.
   Cook over medium heat, thickening the sauce.

6. *Optional:* Remove tofu from sauce and place on a grill to achieve
   grill marks (about 1 minute per side).

7. Serve with Wasabi Sauce.

SEE PHOTO ON PAGE 107

DOS TACOS

4 SERVINGS

Tacos are a Stanford family favorite. We don't use premade taco shells. Joan's cousin Bill, from Wells, British Columbia, showed us that soft homemade tortillas are surprisingly easy to make—you just need masa harina, water, and your palms or a rolling pin or tortilla press. Once you discover how easy it is to make the tortillas, you'll find a variety of uses for them—from tamales to baked corn chips for dipping. Involve your family and friends in making them. Young children enjoy flattening the tortillas in the press and eating the finished project.

This dish is named Dos Tacos because you serve two per person. We stuff them with a mushroom filling and garnish with our sour cream; paired with a large green salad, these tacos help make a hearty, healthy, and simple meal.

FOR THE TORTILLAS

1¾ cups masa harina or yellow corn flour

1 cup plus 2 tablespoons hot water

Wax or parchment paper

FOR THE TACO FILLING AND ASSEMBLY

½ medium yellow onion, chopped

Spray oil or 1 tablespoon olive oil

1 pound cremini mushrooms, cleaned and chopped

½ jalapeño, seeded and chopped

3 cloves garlic, finely chopped

Agave syrup to taste

Salt to taste

Pepper to taste

Shredded cabbage, for garnish

Several sprigs of cilantro, for garnish

Tangy Sour Crème, for garnish (page 262)

Salsa Cruda, for garnish (page 87)

For the Tortillas

1. Mix masa harina and hot water in a medium bowl. Knead until smooth. Let the dough rest for 30 minutes.
2. Divide the dough into golf ball–size balls, and roll them smooth with moistened palms.
3. To make tortillas, either roll out balls with a rolling pin into 4-inch discs, or place each ball between two sheets of wax paper cut to fit a tortilla press, and press out tortilla.
4. Set the tortillas by grilling each side lightly in a skillet or on a griddle over medium heat, for 20–30 seconds per side. Once set, wrap tortillas in a clean towel to maintain moisture, and set aside.

For the Taco Filling and Assembly

1. In a medium sauté pan, add chopped onion and spray oil or olive oil; cook over medium heat for 5–7 minutes or until onions are caramelized.
2. Add cremini mushrooms and jalapeño and continue to sauté.
3. Add chopped garlic, agave, and salt and pepper. Sauté until all moisture is cooked off.
4. Place the filling on warmed tortillas, and top with fresh cabbage and cilantro, Tangy Sour Crème, and Salsa Cruda to serve.

SEA PALM SLIDERS

4-6 SERVINGS

This wholesome, primarily whole-food patty elevates the tiny hamburger popular on many menus. These are no-guilt burgers and can be served without a bun on a shallow bed of lettuce. Don't forget the mustard—or you might try serving with Wasabi Sauce (page 90). At The Ravens, we prefer these served in folded whole wheat flatbread.

---

4 ounces dried sea palm, soaked in water overnight, then drained and chopped

12 ounces white beans, canned or precooked

1 zucchini, grated

2 shallots, diced

2 cloves garlic, minced

1 tablespoon dried thyme

1 tablespoon dried parsley

1 tablespoon salt or to taste

1 teaspoon black pepper

Juice of 1 lemon (about 2 teaspoons)

6 tablespoons organic bread crumbs

2 tablespoons flax meal

2 tablespoons short-grain brown rice, cooked and cooled

Spray oil

1. Preheat oven to 350 degrees.
2. In mixing bowl, combine half of each of the sea palm, white beans, zucchini, shallots, garlic, thyme, parsley, salt, pepper, and lemon juice.
3. In a food processor combine the other half and process until smooth.
4. Fold the contents of the food processor into the mixing bowl, and mix in the bread crumbs, flax meal, and brown rice. Let the mixture cool.
5. Scoop batter using 1–2 tablespoons to create a patty. Place on a baking sheet sprayed lightly with oil and bake for 10 minutes.
6. Flip and bake 10 more minutes. Patties can be refrigerated for future use.
7. To prepare for serving, heat in frying pan sprayed with oil until warm and crisp. Serve with small Whole Wheat Burger Buns (page 69), Dijon mustard, tomatoes, thinly sliced red onion, and arugula.

CRAB-LESS CAKES

4 SERVINGS; 2 CAKES PER PERSON

A few years ago, we entered these crab cakes into a crab-cake contest. We were disqualified because they didn't contain crab! However, one of the judges was staying at the inn and told us that before they were disqualified, our cakes were selected as having the best flavor.

Here's the secret: use Old Bay Seasoning, which is available in most stores. We use organic spices and have worked hard to approximate the taste. Below you'll find our spice mix. If you want the authentic taste, just buy Old Bay Seasoning; it is a very small component of the total dish.

This recipe was principally developed by Barry Horton, who came to The Ravens as an intern from Le Cordon Bleu culinary institute in Portland, Oregon. Barry moved from intern, to employee, to cook, and eventually to chef. You can find Barry and his wife at their restaurant, Sanctuary Bistro, in Berkeley, California. It's well worth a visit. For more information, check out www.sanctuarybistro.com.

FOR THE CRAB-LESS CAKE SEASONING

2 tablespoons celery seed

2 tablespoons black pepper

2 tablespoons red pepper

2 tablespoons dry mustard

1 tablespoon cinnamon

1 tablespoon ginger

FOR THE CRAB-LESS CAKES

2 cups peeled and grated zucchini

1 cup organic bread crumbs

1 cup diced yellow onion

1 cup diced celery

1 tablespoon Crab-less Cake Seasoning (see above)

½ cup Standard Sour Crème (page 262) or Remoulade (page 100), plus more for serving if desired

2 teaspoons vegan Worcestershire sauce

2 teaspoons Dijon mustard

Spray oil

For the Crab-less Cake Seasoning

1. Add all spices to a small bowl and mix thoroughly.

For the Crab-less Cakes

1. Place all ingredients in bowl and mix thoroughly. Let set for 5 minutes.
2. Heat a sauté pan and spray with oil. Form 2-ounce patties of mixture and brown 2 minutes on each side.
3. Serve immediately with Standard Sour Crème or Remoulade.

POTATO LATKES

For some of our friends, latkes are a welcome reminder of grandparents and holidays. For many Americans, the potato pancake is rooted in their past. Latkes remind us of leftover mashed potatoes that our moms turned into potato pancakes.

Latkes are traditionally served with sour cream and applesauce. Play with the variety of potatoes that you use and experiment with the flavor. We enjoy using sweet potatoes because it gives the recipe a bit of sweetness and they are rich in nutrients. You can also experiment with adding fruit and fresh herbs.

---

2 cups peeled and grated sweet potato

2 cups peeled and grated Yukon Gold potato

½ cup potato flour

¼ cup minced shallot

1 tablespoon minced garlic

½ cup canola oil

1 Flax "Egg" (page 256)

Spray oil or 1 tablespoon canola oil

1. Combine all ingredients except oil in a large bowl, and thoroughly incorporate.
2. Measure out ¼-cup scoops of the mixture to form patties.
3. In a heavy frying pan or griddle, heat spray oil or 1 tablespoon canola oil over medium heat.
4. Cook each patty on a griddle or in heavy sauté pan for 2–3 minutes per side, until golden brown.
5. Serve hot.

Note: Try serving with our Standard Sour Crème (page 262).

QUINOA TABBOULEH

MAKES ABOUT 5 CUPS

This is one of our favorite dishes: it is light, minty, and nutritious. As a great variation, fold the tabbouleh into mixed greens, baby greens, or simply torn butter lettuce. It's also great alongside Cauliflower Ceviche (page 114), hummus, crudité, crostini, and homemade baked tortilla chips as hors d'oeuvres for a reception or a healthy Super Bowl party.

---

4 cups cooked and cooled quinoa

6 tomatoes, diced small

3 English cucumbers, diced small

2 cups diced red onion

4 cups finely chopped parsley (about 3 bunches)

1 cup finely chopped mint (about 2 bunches)

Juice of 4 lemons

1 tablespoon golden balsamic vinegar

Salt and pepper to taste

¼–½ cup olive oil

1. Combine quinoa, vegetables, herbs, lemon juice, vinegar, and salt and pepper in a large bowl.
2. Add olive oil in ¼-cup increments, until the quinoa sticks together and tastes creamy.

ROASTED CORN RELISH OR SIDE

MAKES ABOUT 4 CUPS

Here's a versatile take on corn: Served hot, it's a side. Serve cold, it's a relish. This dish is a staff favorite.

We prepare this relish with frozen corn kernels in the winter and in the summer, fresh corn off the cob. To remove the kernels from a fresh ear of corn, slide a sharp knife between the cob and the kernels.

---

2 cups sweet corn kernels

½ cup diced red bell pepper

¼ cup diced yellow onion

2 tablespoons seeded and minced jalapeño

2 tablespoons minced cilantro

Salt and pepper to taste

Juice of 2 limes

1. Preheat oven to 425 degrees.
2. Place corn kernels on a baking sheet in a single layer and bake for 8–10 minutes, stirring every 2–3 minutes, until they begin to brown slightly.
3. In a bowl, combine corn, bell pepper, onion, jalapeño, and cilantro and mix thoroughly. Add salt and pepper.
4. Mix in lime juice before serving. Serve hot or cold.

RAVENS BRAISED GREENS

2-4 SERVINGS

These greens can stand on their own; be served as a side dish; or placed on top of rice, noodles, or quinoa. Those on special diets often order this dish as an entrée with brown rice. It is intensely nutritious, full of fiber, vitamins, minerals, and antioxidants. The vegetable stock allows the natural flavors of the chard and kale to explode in your mouth.

½ cup Ravens All-Purpose Vegetable Stock (page 163) or store-bought vegan broth

1 bunch (about ½ pound) rainbow chard, cleaned, stemmed, and chopped into bite-size pieces

1 bunch (about ½ pound) kale, cleaned, stemmed, and chopped into bite-size pieces

2 cloves garlic, minced (optional)

½ teaspoon salt

1. In a large sauté pan, combine vegetable stock, rainbow chard, kale, and garlic. Cover and cook over medium heat until greens have steamed and wilted.
2. Season with salt and mix well.

ROSEMARY ROASTED POTATO WEDGES

4-6 SERVINGS

Potato wedges have been on our menu for years. They are The Ravens' version of fries. When baking, be sure to separate the potatoes. Avoid overcrowding in the oven or when using a toaster oven. You want a "dry" oven to ensure the potatoes crisp nicely rather than steam. Rosemary is a great spice on these wedges, as it is rejuvenating, anti-inflammatory, and delicious.

---

4 red-skinned potatoes, washed and cut into wedges

2 tablespoons minced rosemary

4 cloves garlic, crushed

1 tablespoon canola oil

1 tablespoon olive oil

Salt and pepper to taste

1. Preheat oven to 350 degrees.
2. In a mixing bowl, toss potatoes, rosemary, and garlic with the oils.
3. Evenly spread potatoes on a baking sheet. Sprinkle lightly with salt and pepper.
4. Bake potatoes, turning after 45 minutes. Continue baking for a total of 60–75 minutes, or until tender and golden brown.
5. Serve warm. If the potatoes cool, reheat for 10 minutes in a 400-degree oven.

SALADS & DRESSINGS

We love salads at the Stanford Inn! We grow much of the produce and herbs that go into our salads and dressings, especially the rarer ingredients usually not found in the produce aisle of the grocery store. Each season we change the menu according to availability, and this allows us to offer a large range of exciting and satisfying salads.

We serve our salads with pride—and for good reason. In addition to many varieties of lettuces, we use a unique selection of wild greens that are medicine for the body and soul. They come from our garden to the kitchen, and are freshly picked every day.

We also grow edible flowers and use them in salads as a component as, for example, a grated carrot. Flowers garnish our plates and flavor the water served at our tables. Consider using them on green salads to add a dramatic splash of color and delicate, nutty flavors. Flowers are reservoirs for all that is good in plants. (Caution: Only use organically grown flowers to avoid pesticides used in many gardens. A list of some of the flowers we use follows on page 141. If in doubt about the edibility of any flower or plant, don't eat it!)

MAKE YOUR OWN SALAD

Mix these greens and flowers with conventional lettuces, and top with any of our dressings to create a seasonal salad with a variety of flavors and textures. *Note:* For those plants that are less common, we have provided botanical names.

GREENS

Arugula: A European green in the radish family. Tastes like a combination of peanuts and radish.

Calendula: A sweet yellow/orange flower that can substitute for salad greens and that is good for the skin.

Endive: A member of the chicory family that has a slightly bitter yet fresh flavor, and is a good digestive tonic. Because of its shape and stiffness, Belgian endive is a life-supportive replacement for potato and corn chips for dips.

Huizontle (*Chenopodium nuttaliae*): A Mexican wild delicacy that tastes like a cross between spinach and young broccoli.

Wild Kale and Lacinato Kale: A green that is is high in calcium, beta-carotene, and other antioxidants.

Mâche/Corn Lettuce (*Valerianella locusta*): A European green in the valerian family, which has calming properties. This green tastes like young corn.

Miner's Lettuce (*Claytonia perfoliata*): A green native to the West Coast that has a mild flavor similar to spinach.

Minutina (*Plantago coronopus*): In the plantain family; an all-around healing herb, aiding digestion and cleansing the system. Mild flavor.

New Zealand Spinach (*Tetragonia expansa*): Another California native that tastes like spinach.

Sorrel (*Rumex acetosa*): A green with a bright tart flavor.

EDIBLE FLOWERS

Flowers contain antioxidants and anti-inflammatory compounds, as well as a variety of vitamins and chemicals that fight cancer. For example, nasturtiums contain cancer-fighting lycopene and lutein. We maintain that eating a varied plant-based diet, including flowers, will help assure health and well-being. A variety of flowers should be included as condiments in salads.

Bachelor Buttons
Calendula
Carnations
Clove Pinks
Fuchsia
Gladiolas (remove anthers)
Jasmine
Lavender
Marigolds

Mint and
Chocolate Mint Geranium
Nasturtium
Pansy
Passion Flower
Pineapple Guava
Rose
Snapdragon
Viola

The above list is only a partial one. Because flowers can hold pesticides, be absolutely certain that your flowers are organic and grown to be eaten. Do not use flowers that were grown for arranging.

HERBS

Like flowers, herbs are rich in healthful properties and add flavor to our dishes.

Anise Hyssop
Borage
Catnip
Chamomile
Chervil
Chives
Cilantro
Dill
Fennel
Garlic Chives

Hyssop
Lemon Verbena
Marjoram
Mints
Oregano
Rosemary
Sages
Savories
Thyme

SALAD NAPOLEON

4–6 SERVINGS

An artful salad for special occasions. Although optional, the basil chiffonade adds color and flavor. And there's plenty of flavor with the béchamel and pesto. The optional balsamic or olive oil drizzle is for those who like the taste of either, but they aren't necessary. We love this salad, which can serve as an entrée, because of the textures of the raw vegetables and flavors.

FOR THE SUN-DRIED TOMATO PESTO

¾ cup sun-dried tomatoes, soaked and drained

¼ cup pumpkin seeds, soaked and drained

¼ cup tightly packed basil

1 tablespoon balsamic vinegar

3 tablespoons olive oil

1 teaspoon salt

¼ teaspoon black pepper

FOR THE NAPOLEONS AND ASSEMBLY

3 large heirloom tomatoes, sliced ¼ inch thick

1 cup Sun-Dried Tomato Pesto (see above)

1 zucchini, sliced thin using mandoline

1¼ cups Cashew Béchamel (page 81)

1 large beet, peeled and sliced paper-thin using mandoline or sushi knife

1 bunch (about 4 ounces) basil leaves, chiffonade (optional)

Olive oil or Balsamic Reduction (page 92), for drizzling (optional)

For the Sun-Dried Tomato Pesto

1. In food processor, combine sun-dried tomatoes, pumpkin seeds, basil, and balsamic vinegar. Process until well combined.
2. Slowly stream in olive oil and process until smooth. Add salt and pepper and process a final time.

For the Napoleons and Assembly

1. Lay 1 slice of tomato on plate and top with about 2 tablespoons of the Sun-Dried Tomato Pesto.
2. Cover tomato with sliced zucchini. (If slicing lengthwise, zucchini may need to be cut in half.) Top with about 2 tablespoons of the Cashew Béchamel.
3. Cover zucchini with slices of beet. Top with about 2 tablespoons tomato pesto.
4. Stack more vegetables and spread as desired.
5. Garnish with chiffonade basil and drizzle with olive oil or Balsamic Reduction.
6. Repeat to make 4–6 salads.

CHANTERELLE WALDORF SALAD

4-6 SERVINGS

This is a Mendocino woodland twist on the classic apple-based Waldorf salad. Our mothers might have served this rich salad as their principal dish during their biweekly bridge club luncheons (think 1960s). We find it interesting that both our moms were great bridge players but they never played with or against each other.

We serve our Chanterelle Waldorf Salad during the mushroom festival held in November. With all the nutrient-dense ingredients, we keep the portions small so that our diners can enjoy the main course and wine pairings. A dry Mendocino Gewürztraminer pairs well, by the way.

---

1 tablespoon olive oil

6 cups cleaned and finely diced chanterelle or other preferred mushrooms (e.g., oyster, cremini, hedgehog, portobello)

1½ teaspoons salt, divided

1 apple, peeled and diced small

¼ cup diced onion

¼ cup raisins

¼ cup diced celery

12.3 ounces silken tofu

1 shallot, roughly chopped

½ teaspoon pepper

2 tablespoons apple cider vinegar

1 tablespoon Dijon mustard

1 tablespoon agave syrup

4–6 cups mixed baby greens or mixed garden lettuce, torn into bite-size pieces

¼ cup toasted walnuts

1. In large sauté pan, heat oil over medium-high heat and add mushrooms. Cook until golden brown and tender, for about 10 minutes. (If pan is too crowded with mushrooms, they may not brown. To avoid this, cook in batches.) Add ¼ teaspoon of the salt and mix further. Drain any excess liquid. Let cool.

2. In large mixing bowl, combine cooked mushrooms, apple, onion, raisins, and celery. Set aside.

3. In high-speed blender, combine silken tofu, shallot, remaining 1¼ teaspoons salt, pepper, apple cider vinegar, Dijon mustard, and agave. Puree until completely smooth.

4. Pour tofu mixture over mushroom and vegetable medley. Mix well.

5. Season with additional salt and pepper as desired.

6. Per serving, place about 1 cup greens on plate and top with ½ cup chanterelle mixture. Sprinkle with toasted walnuts and serve.

GRILLED PEAR OR PEACH SALAD WITH THYME VERJUS DRESSING ON WILTED SPINACH

6–8 SERVINGS

This is one of our favorite salads! Grilled fruit enlivens virtually any salad. We offer the option of peaches or pears because they ripen in different seasons. However, don't limit yourself; these fruits are just a starting point. Nectarines are wonderful with the Thyme Verjus Dressing, as is grilled melon, cantaloupe, honeydew, watermelon, figs, and apples. If you have never grilled fruit before, now is the time. Enjoy!

FOR THE THYME VERJUS DRESSING

2 shallots, minced

3 tablespoons (about ½ bunch) stemmed and chopped fresh thyme

Salt to taste

½ cup Verjus wine (Navarro Vineyards' tart grape juice)

¾ cup olive oil

FOR THE WILTED SPINACH

1 cup Thyme Verjus Dressing (see previous)

6–8 cups baby spinach

FOR THE MARINATED RED ONIONS

1 cup rice vinegar

1 tablespoon agave syrup

½ teaspoon salt

2 red onions, sliced into half-moons

FOR THE GRILLED PEAR OR PEACH

3–4 pears or peaches (see note)

Spray oil

Salt to taste

FOR THE PEPITA GARNISH

1 cup raw pumpkin seeds

1 teaspoon salt

½ teaspoon chili powder

1 tablespoon olive oil

For the Thyme Verjus Dressing

1. Combine shallots, thyme, salt, and wine in a medium mixing bowl and mix well.
2. Slowly stream in oil until well mixed.

For the Wilted Spinach

1. In large frying pan over medium heat, heat dressing until it is hot.
2. Toss in spinach, let it wilt, then turn the heat off, tossing the hot dressing and spinach with tongs.

For the Marinated Red Onions

1. Mix vinegar, agave, and salt together in a medium bowl.
2. Add onions and let sit for at least 20 minutes.

For the Grilled Pear or Peach

1. Cut fruit in half, and remove pit or core.

2. Lightly spray with oil and dust with salt.
3. Grill until grill marks appear.
4. Slice three-fourths of the way through the fruit and serve fanned.

For the Pepita Garnish

1. Preheat oven to 350 degrees.
2. Mix all ingredients on a baking sheet.
3. Bake for 10–15 minutes, until brown.

For the Assembly

1. Place wilted spinach on a salad plate.
2. Fan half of a grilled peach or pear in front at one corner of the plate.
3. Place marinated onions in the middle on top.
4. Sprinkle salad with toasted pepitas.

Pears or Peaches Note: If fruit is not soft, place in oven and bake at 350 degrees until soft.

SHIITAKE MUSHROOM SALAD

4-6 SERVINGS

For many years we have worked with naturalists, Chinese herbal practitioners, mycologists, and nutritionists to create recipes that provide culinary "doses" of helpful plants and fungi. This salad was first introduced as a medicinal mushroom salad.

Shiitake mushrooms' medicinal properties include antitumor and antiviral effects, and they help lower serum cholesterol and enhance the immune system. Arugula and napa cabbage enhance shiitake's cancer-fighting ability with sulfur-containing compounds, especially sulforaphane. Sulforaphane also provides the bitterness in arugula that contrasts with the fruit and mirin in this salad.

FOR THE SALAD BASE

1 small napa cabbage, shredded

½ cup baby arugula

1 carrot, chiffonade or fine julienne

3 scallions, thinly sliced

8–10 large shiitake mushrooms, cut in half

1 tablespoon sunflower oil

Salt and pepper to taste

1 tablespoon mirin cooking wine

FOR THE GINGER MISO DRESSING

¼ cup chopped onion

2 tablespoons peeled and sliced fresh ginger

2½ cloves garlic, smashed

1 teaspoon sesame oil

1 teaspoon olive oil

2 tablespoons miso paste

Salt to taste (optional)

3 tablespoons mirin cooking wine

2 tablespoons maple syrup

1½ tablespoons brown rice vinegar

2 tablespoons water

FOR THE ASSEMBLY

1 red bell pepper, chiffonade or fine julienne

1 kohlrabi (or peeled broccoli stem), chiffonade or fine julienne

1 orange, peeled and segmented

1 bunch (about 4 ounces) chives, chopped

For the Salad Base

1. Mix cabbage, baby arugula, carrot, and scallions in a large bowl.
2. In a sauté pan, sauté shiitake mushrooms with sunflower oil, salt, and pepper over medium heat for about 10 minutes or until golden brown.
3. Deglaze pan with mirin cooking wine.

For the Ginger Miso Dressing

1. In a sauté pan or small saucepan, combine onion, ginger, garlic, and oils. Cook over medium heat until onion is softened, about 7 minutes. Cool.
2. Using high-speed blender, puree the cooled mixture with remaining ingredients except water.
3. Slowly stream in water and blend until smooth and creamy.

For the Assembly

1. Toss the salad base in 3 tablespoons of dressing.
2. Place 1 tablespoon of the dressing on bottom of each serving plate.
3. Place 1 cup of the salad base in center of plate; pile high.
4. Place red bell pepper, kohlrabi, and orange segments around the cabbage.
5. Place sautéed mushrooms on top of the cabbage and carrot mixture.
6. Garnish with chives.

HEIRLOOM TOMATO SALAD

2-4 SERVINGS

Beginning in early spring, usually April, heirloom tomatoes arrive at our door and continue to grow for seven months. Heirlooms ripened on the vine are varied and delicious. For a rainbow of color on the plate, we mix green-purple, red, orange, and yellow heirlooms with a gentle drizzle of white balsamic vinaigrette, interweaving their flavors and literally providing our first taste of summer.

FOR THE WHITE BALSAMIC AND LIME VINAIGRETTE

Zest of 1 lime

½ cup lime juice

3 tablespoons white balsamic vinegar

1 tablespoon agave syrup

½ cup olive oil

2 teaspoons minced fresh basil

Dash of yellow mustard powder

Salt and pepper to taste

FOR THE SALAD BASE

4 cups mixed baby greens

2 large or 3–4 smaller heirloom tomatoes, sliced if large or quartered if small

2 fresh or dried figs, cut into wedges

2 basil leaves, chiffonade

For the White Balsamic and Lime Vinaigrette

1. In a stainless steel bowl, whisk together the lime zest, lime juice, white balsamic vinegar, and agave.
2. Whisk in olive oil until emulsified.
3. Whisk in basil and mustard powder, and add salt and pepper to taste. Set aside.

For the Salad Base

1. Mix greens and tomato slices with vinaigrette.
2. Arrange the greens in the middle of each serving plate with the tomatoes around the greens.
3. Garnish with fig wedges and chiffonade basil.

KALE SALAD WITH AVOCADO LIME VERJUS DRESSING, TRUMPET MUSHROOMS, AND AVOCADO

4–6 SERVINGS

This is Jeff's favorite salad. The ingredients are amazing, and the salad is filling. We stack the components in a cylindrical mold, but you can also push them into a large "bucket" glass used for cocktails, or a shallow wineglass to achieve the same shape.

This is not a "raw" dish: the mushrooms must be thoroughly cooked to remove any toxic elements and provide access to their health-promoting compounds. Cauliflower Ceviche (page 114) can be substituted for the Mushroom Ceviche to qualify this salad as totally raw.

FOR THE KALE SALAD AND AVOCADO LIME VERJUS DRESSING

1 bunch (about ½ pound) kale, chiffonade (can substitute romaine lettuce)

1 teaspoon salt

2 ripe avocados, peeled and pitted

½ cup tightly packed cilantro

Juice of 1 lime

Salt and pepper to taste

2 tablespoons Verjus (Navarro Vineyards' tart grape juice)

1 tablespoon brown rice vinegar

1 tablespoon agave syrup

¼ cup raisins

FOR THE MUSHROOM CEVICHE AND ASSEMBLY

4 cups trumpet royale mushrooms, cleaned and then sliced into rounds

¼ cup water or Ravens All-Purpose Vegetable Stock (page 163) or store-bought vegan broth

1 shallot, minced

1 jalapeño, seeded and minced (optional)

1 tablespoon minced fresh thyme

1 teaspoon salt

Juice of 2 lemons

Juice of 2 limes

Juice of 1 orange

1 avocado, peeled, pitted, and thinly sliced

1 red bell pepper, seeded and diced

For the Kale Salad and Avocado Lime Verjus Dressing

1. Place chiffonade kale in a large bowl and sprinkle with salt.
2. Massage the salt into kale leaves until they are well coated. This process will help break down the cell wall of the kale, making it tender. If using romaine lettuce, omit this step.
3. Combine the avocados, cilantro, lime juice, salt and pepper, Verjus, brown rice vinegar, and agave in a high-speed blender, and mix until completely smooth.
4. Combine raisins and 2 tablespoons of the dressing with kale and set aside.

For the Mushroom Ceviche and Assembly

1. Braise mushrooms over medium heat with ¼ cup of water or vegetable stock to help prevent sticking. Stir occasionally until mushrooms are cooked through, about 10 minutes. Drain.
2. Combine mushrooms, shallot, jalapeño, thyme, salt, and citrus juices in large bowl and mix until well combined.
3. Let sit for at least 3 hours to incorporate flavors.
4. For each salad, in a cylinder mold on a salad plate, insert about 3 inches of the massaged and dressed kale, pressing down firmly.
5. Follow with a thin layer of the sautéed mushrooms.
6. Finish with a layer of thinly sliced avocados fanned out on top.
7. Remove mold. Garnish with the diced red bell peppers.

RAVENS CAESAR SALAD

4-6 SERVINGS

Obviously not the original Caesar, which contains egg yolks, Parmesan cheese, and anchovies, this recipe still captures the zest and richness of the original. You can add vegan Parmesan, but the nutritional yeast in the dressing provides a Parmesan flavor.

FOR THE CAESAR DRESSING

6.5 ounces silken tofu

½ cup minced cooked onion

¼ cup capers

¼ cup white miso

1 tablespoon nutritional yeast

1 tablespoon chopped roasted garlic

1 tablespoon minced raw garlic

¼ cup lemon juice

3 tablespoons Dijon mustard

2 tablespoons vegan Worcestershire sauce

1 tablespoon white wine vinegar

1½ cups olive oil

½ tablespoon toasted and crumbled nori

Salt and pepper to taste

FOR THE CROUTONS

Fresh bread, whole or partial loaf, torn into ½- to ¾-inch pieces (1 cup of torn bread will provide croutons for 6 servings)

2 tablespoons olive oil or organic spray olive oil

FOR THE SALAD BASE AND ASSEMBLY

1–2 tablespoons olive oil or organic spray olive oil

1 lemon, cut in half, divided

2 cloves garlic, cut in half

3 romaine hearts, leaves separated and not torn (they should be whole and crisp)

½ tablespoon toasted and crumbled nori

For the Caesar Dressing

1. In a blender, place tofu, onion, capers, miso, nutritional yeast, both garlics, lemon juice, mustard, Worcestershire sauce, and vinegar and blend until smooth.
2. With the blender running, slowly add oil to emulsify.
3. Transfer to a stainless steel bowl and fold in nori powder.
4. Season with salt and pepper to taste. Refrigerate until ready to use.

For the Croutons

1. Preheat oven to 375 degrees.
2. Toss torn bread in olive oil and spread on baking sheet, or spread on baking sheet and spray one side with olive oil, turn over, and spray again.
3. Bake for 10 minutes, turning at least once, or until turning golden.

For the Salad Base and Assembly

1. Wipe a large salad bowl (preferably wooden) with olive oil or spray with oil.
2. Rub ½ lemon on inside of salad bowl. Then rub salad bowl with garlic cloves.
3. Place romaine leaves and croutons into the bowl and toss with Caesar Dressing.
4. Sprinkle salad with the nori powder, slice remaining lemon half into rounds, and place over the salad.

RAVENS ROASTED BEET SALAD

4-6 SERVINGS

After the Ravens Caesar Salad (page 154), our most popular salad is this beet salad. It is definitely Joan's favorite, and if you're a beet lover, this one's for you. Jeff likes the dressing and frisée, but he's not a fan of beets. A note about frisée: it is bitter and contrasts well with the beets and the slight sweetness of the dressing. Nevertheless, you may want to mix in baby salad greens or replace the frisée entirely if you don't like bitter greens. If you love beets you can skip the pâté or just sprinkle with walnuts.

Beets grow well on the coast. They are hardy and relatively trouble free. As a result, we will always be serving some version of beet salad.

The walnut pâté recipe can be halved, and it can be served on crostini as an appetizer.

FOR THE ROASTED SHALLOT VINAIGRETTE

4–5 shallots, roasted

¾–1 cup golden balsamic vinegar

1½ tablespoons Dijon mustard

1 teaspoon agave syrup

Salt and pepper to taste

1½ cups olive oil

FOR THE WALNUT PÂTÉ

2 cups toasted walnuts

Zest and juice of 2 lemons

1 tablespoon nutritional yeast

2 teaspoons salt

FOR THE ROASTED BEETS

4–5 yellow and/or red beets

1 tablespoon olive oil

½ teaspoon salt

FOR THE ASSEMBLY

4–6 cups of frisée, baby lettuce greens, or mixture of both

For the Roasted Shallot Vinaigrette

1. Add shallots, vinegar, Dijon mustard, agave, and salt and pepper to a high-speed blender. Blend until smooth.
2. Stream in olive oil slowly and blend further to emulsify all ingredients.

For the Walnut Pâté

1. In a food processor, pulse toasted walnuts until well chopped.
2. Add lemon zest and juice, nutritional yeast, and salt and continue to process until a paste is achieved.

For the Roasted Beets

1. Preheat the oven to 425 degrees.
2. Wash and scrub beets well and cut off tops and bottoms.
3. Toss the beets with the olive oil and salt.
4. Place yellow beets on one sheet tray and red beets on another sheet tray and cover both with foil. Roast for 40–60 minutes, until tender (cooking time varies depending on beet color).
5. Cool and slice.

For the Assembly

1. For each salad, mix greens with 1 tablespoon of vinaigrette. Place in a pile in the middle of a plate.
2. Fan beet slices around the greens.
3. Mold a heaping tablespoon of walnut pâté into an ovoid shape. You can use your hands or if using restaurant protocol, mold using 2 tablespoons to shape the pâté. If you prefer, just spoon out a heaping tablespoon on top of the greens.

VALENTINE'S POACHED PEAR AND GRILLED ENDIVE SALAD

4 SERVINGS

Winter is the time for salad with poached pear, whose sweetness contrasts beautifully with bitter frisée. For Valentine's Day we poach pears in red wine, which creates a deep red color, associated with passion. Our poaching liquid contains cinnamon, which is used in many so-called aphrodisiac preparations. Cinnamon aids in digestion—a bloated feeling is not particularly conducive to romantic evenings. Finally, the shape of the pear is symbolic of fertility (check out the pear-shaped pregnant abdomens of Marija Gimbutas's female figurines from her archeological digs and contemporary tribal African carvings).

This salad was featured in *Vegetarian Times* in January 2012.

FOR THE POACHED PEARS

2 Bosc pears, peeled and cut in half lengthwise

2–3 cloves

1 cinnamon stick

1½ cups red wine or apple juice

¼ cup agave syrup

Zest and juice of 1 lemon

FOR THE DRESSING

½ teaspoon salt

Pinch of ground black pepper

2 tablespoons balsamic vinegar

2 tablespoons maple syrup or agave syrup

2 tablespoons extra-virgin olive oil

FOR THE SALAD BASE AND ASSEMBLY

4 red endive hearts

1 medium head (about 5 cups) frisée or other leafy green, cleaned and trimmed

2 scallions, cut into slivers on the bias

For the Poached Pears

1. In a saucepan, combine pears, cloves, cinnamon stick, wine, agave, and lemon zest and juice.
2. Bring mixture to a boil over high heat, then reduce heat to low and allow pears to poach for 25 minutes, until fork tender. Be sure to spoon liquid over pear halves occasionally.
3. Remove pears from liquid and set aside to cool. Reserve excess liquid.
4. Once cooled, cut each half in half again lengthwise.

For the Dressing

1. In mixing bowl, combine salt, pepper, balsamic vinegar, maple syrup, and olive oil, and whisk gently.

For the Salad Base and Assembly

1. Cut endive hearts in half lengthwise and brush dressing over each piece, reserving excess for later.
2. Using an indoor grill pan, heat it well and brush with oil. Cook endive hearts, cut-side down, for approximately 5 minutes, until slightly wilted.
3. Drizzle remaining dressing over frisée and scallions and place on salad plates.
4. Fan pear slices around the greens.
5. Place endives around the salad and garnish with leftover dressing and/or remaining poaching liquid.

POTATO SALAD

4 SERVINGS

This is a great potato salad that is wonderful in the summer. The coolness and tanginess of the dressing is a great complement to a spicy barbecue. The capers provide a sophisticated zip.

---

5 unpeeled red-skinned potatoes, cut into 1–1¼-inch cubes, or small new potatoes, cut into ½-inch cubes

6 ounces silken tofu

1 teaspoon minced garlic

2 tablespoons Dijon mustard

Juice of 3 lemons

¼ cup diced red onion

¼ cup capers

2 tablespoons minced fresh dill

Salt and white pepper

1. Place potatoes in a large pot and cover with water. Bring to a boil and cook for 12–15 minutes, until the potatoes are fork tender. Strain and let cool. Do not overcook; potatoes should be tender, but not mushy.

2. In a high-speed blender, blend tofu, garlic, mustard, and lemon juice until smooth. Transfer to a bowl.

3. Add onion, capers, dill, and cooled potatoes to the tofu mixture and toss until well coated.

4. Season with salt and white pepper to taste.

5. Serve cold.

ASIAN SESAME SLAW

We serve this salad with our Trumpet Royale or Tofu Satay with Peanut Sauce
(page 113), but it can also stand on its own as a light lunch.

FOR THE DRESSING

2 tablespoons brown sugar

1½ tablespoons
chopped cilantro

½ tablespoon chopped garlic

1 small jalapeño, seeded

¾-inch slice fresh ginger

¾ cup orange juice

2 tablespoons rice vinegar

1¼ tablespoons sesame oil

1 tablespoon tamari

¼ cup expeller-pressed
canola oil

¼ cup white sesame seeds

2 tablespoons black
sesame seeds

FOR THE VEGETABLE
MIXTURE AND ASSEMBLY

½ large head (about
1 pound) green cabbage

½ large head
(about 1 pound) red cabbage

3 large carrots

1 bunch (about 4 ounces)
scallions

For the Dressing

1. In a food processor, combine brown sugar, cilantro, garlic, jalapeño, ginger, orange juice, vinegar, sesame oil, and tamari; pulse to mix.
2. As you slowly pulse, drizzle in the canola oil to emulsify the dressing.
3. Remove from the food processor and stir in the sesame seeds.

For the Vegetable Mixture and Assembly

1. Shred all of the vegetables using the shredding blade on your food processor or a cheese grater.
2. Mix well and add dressing according to taste.

SOUPS

Until The Ravens opened, we were of two minds regarding soup. Jeff never ordered soup; Joan almost always did. Jeff had one specialty soup—a wonderful vegan Broccoli Soup with Spinach (page 184) that Alex and Kate loved. But we rarely served soup at home.

Soup is a restaurant staple and once we had a restaurant, we made and served soup. What was needed, of course, was to create soups that appealed to Jeff every night. So over the first few years we were challenged to create fresh and exciting soups that could be considered meals in themselves.

When making soup at home, it is important to have a hardworking blender. Most restaurants that serve creamy soups use heavy cream from the dairy, but we make our "heavy cream" with a smooth puree of broccoli stems, potatoes, grains including oats and brown rice, and nuts, particularly cashews.

To make the broccoli stem puree, we peel away the green fibrous outer stem, which holds most of the broccoli flavor, slice the remaining core into disks, either boil or steam the disks until tender, and then puree them with only enough stock to create a cream. The broccoli cream can be frozen for future use.

RAVENS ALL-PURPOSE VEGETABLE STOCK

We begin this section with our vegetable stock, which is used as a base in many of the following soups. Be sure to use organic ingredients; any of the vegetables can hold traces of pesticides and herbicides, especially carrots and celery. If you make more than you can use, freeze in pint batches for future use.

2 carrots, peeled and cut into ½-inch pieces

2 onions, cut into ¼-inch pieces

2 leeks, both white and green parts, cleaned and sliced

2 stalks celery, cut into ½-inch pieces

3 cloves garlic, cut in half

2 parsnips, peeled and cut into ½-inch pieces

1 cup chopped parsley (approximately 1 bunch)

4 quarts water

4 sprigs fresh thyme or 2 teaspoons dried thyme

1 bay leaf

1 tablespoon black peppercorns

1 teaspoon sea salt

1. In a stockpot, combine carrots, onions, leeks, celery, garlic, parsnips, parsley, and water. Bring to a boil over high heat.

2. Turn heat to low and add thyme, bay leaf, peppercorns, and salt. Simmer, covered, for 1 hour.

3. Allow stock to cool, and then strain through a medium-mesh strainer into a clean pot or heat-resistant container and refrigerate until ready to use.

Options: Depending on what type of soup you are making, you may want to add any of the following to the stock while simmering:

- *5 Roma tomatoes, cut in half*
- *1 potato or sweet potato, peeled and sliced*
- *1 chopped fennel bulb with top*
- *1 cup mushroom stems or 16 ounces white mushrooms, cut in half*

RED DAHL

6 SERVINGS

Many soups are better the second day, but we have yet to find out whether this is true for this Red Dahl; it does not last long enough! This soup was created by one of our most enthusiastic interns, Rebecca Katz, who was referred to us by the Natural Gourmet Institute in New York City. Today she creates recipes that help heal those challenged by disease.

FOR THE LENTILS

4 cups red lentils, rinsed well
1 teaspoon turmeric
½ teaspoon ground cumin
1 cinnamon stick

FOR THE CURRY MIXTURE AND SOUP ASSEMBLY

1½ tablespoons canola oil
1 teaspoon yellow mustard seeds
1 cup sliced leeks
½ cup chopped golden raisins
2 tablespoons chopped ginger
1 teaspoon ground cumin
1 teaspoon ground coriander
½–1 teaspoon red pepper flakes to taste
½ teaspoon fenugreek
½ teaspoon cardamom
½ teaspoon turmeric
1 cinnamon stick
1 cup Ravens All-Purpose Vegetable Stock (page 163) or store-bought vegan broth
½ can (about 3 ounces) organic tomato paste
½ cup chopped cilantro
1 (13.6-ounce) can coconut milk
2–3 tablespoons agave syrup
Salt to taste
Lemon juice to taste

For the Lentils

1. Place lentils into a 6-quart pot and add water to cover lentils by 5 inches.
2. Bring to a boil, stirring occasionally to prevent lentils from sticking or burning.
3. The lentils will foam, and as foam rises, remove it with a slotted spoon and discard.
4. Once foaming subsides, add remaining ingredients, reduce heat to medium-low, and simmer, uncovered, for 20–30 minutes, or until the lentils have broken down and thickened. The mixture should resemble a thin paste. Remove cinnamon stick. Set aside.

For the Curry Mixture and Soup Assembly

1. Heat oil in a large sauté pan and add mustard seeds, heating until they pop.
2. Add leeks, raisins, ginger, cumin, coriander, red pepper flakes, fenugreek, cardamom, turmeric, and cinnamon stick and sauté for 5 minutes.
3. Add vegetable stock and tomato paste. Simmer for 2–3 minutes.
4. Add remaining ingredients except the salt and lemon juice and stir to thoroughly incorporate.
5. Remove cinnamon stick from the mixture.
6. Combine curry mixture with the cooked lentils.
7. Blend the mixture in small batches in a high-speed blender until smooth.
8. Add salt, lemon juice, and additional agave to taste.
9. Serve warm.

ROASTED FENNEL AND CANNELLINI BEAN SOUP WITH GARLIC AND SAGE

4–6 SERVINGS

Fennel grows abundantly in our gardens. We are always looking for ways to use this nutritious and very tangy vegetable. In this soup the flavor of the fennel is subtle, blending well with the rosemary and thyme.

---

2 cups dried cannellini beans, soaked overnight

7 cloves garlic, divided

2 sprigs fresh rosemary

2 sprigs fresh thyme

2 stalks fennel frond, divided

4 tablespoons plus 1 teaspoon olive oil, divided

1½ teaspoons salt, divided, plus more to taste

6 fennel bulbs, sliced lengthwise, hearts intact

1¼ tablespoons finely chopped sage, divided

¼ teaspoon pepper, plus more to taste

1 medium yellow onion, chopped

1 leek, white part only, cleaned and chopped

1 shallot, chopped

¼ teaspoon dried thyme

1 teaspoon cane juice

¼ cup white wine

8 cups Ravens All-Purpose Vegetable Stock (page 163) or store-bought vegan broth

1 cup stemmed and chopped parsley

2 tablespoons lemon juice

1. Preheat oven to 400 degrees.
2. Rinse and drain the soaked beans and place in a 4-quart pot. Add enough water to cover the beans by 3 inches.
3. Using cheesecloth, make a sachet with 4 cloves of the garlic, rosemary, thyme, and 1 frond of the fennel. Add to the beans along with 1 teaspoon of the olive oil.
4. Bring the beans to a boil, reduce heat, and simmer for 1 hour.
5. Add 1 teaspoon of the salt to the beans and continue cooking until tender, about 30 minutes longer.
6. On a lightly greased sheet pan, brush fennel bulbs with 2 tablespoons of the olive oil, 1 tablespoon of the sage, and salt and pepper to taste. Roast for 15–20 minutes, or until golden and tender.
7. In a 4-quart saucepan, heat remaining 2 tablespoons olive oil over medium heat. Add onion, leek, and shallot, and sauté 5 minutes, until soft and translucent.
8. Finely chop remaining 3 cloves garlic. Add chopped garlic, dried thyme, remaining ¼ tablespoon sage, remaining ¼ teaspoon pepper, remaining ½ teaspoon salt, and cane juice. Sauté for 2 more minutes.
9. Deglaze pan with white wine. Allow the wine to evaporate, then add stock and 1 remaining fennel frond and simmer for 20 minutes. Remove the fennel frond.
10. Combine vegetable stock, onion mixture, beans, roasted fennel, and parsley and blend in small batches in a high-speed blender until smooth.
11. Strain soup through a chinois to achieve a satiny texture.
12. Add lemon juice, and season with salt and pepper to taste.

SUMMER SWEET CORN BISQUE

4-6 SERVINGS

Here is a wonderful, creamy summer bisque with the fresh flavor of corn—we even use the cobs! Cashews are blended and liquefied to add a creamy taste that diners claim must be from heavy dairy cream. Although cashews contain fat, remember no plant or seed has cholesterol.

This soup, as much as any other item on our menu, reflects our desire to nourish and satisfy.

---

3 dozen cobs corn (remove and reserve kernels)

8 cups Ravens All-Purpose Vegetable Stock (page 163) or store-bought vegan broth

1 cup raw cashews

¼ cup olive oil

5 yellow onions, diced medium

½ cup white wine

Salt and pepper to taste

10 cloves roasted garlic

Basil oil or slow-roasted corn kernels, for garnish (see notes; optional)

1. Place all the corn cobs (with kernels already removed) in a stockpot. Cover with vegetable stock and cook over medium heat, covered, for 30 minutes.
2. Strain the mixture and discard the cobs, reserving the stock.
3. In a high-speed blender, blend cashews with 4 cups of the stock until smooth. Set aside.
4. Place oil and onions in a large sauté pan and sauté 5 minutes, until translucent. Deglaze the pan with the white wine and reduce until it is almost dry.
5. Add remaining 4 cups reserved stock and corn kernels to the onion mixture and season with salt and pepper. Simmer for 30 minutes, or until the corn kernels are soft.
6. Blend corn and onion mixture and roasted garlic in a high-speed blender until smooth. Strain mixture through a chinois to ensure smooth, velvety texture and to remove the tough parts of the corn kernels.
7. Stir cashew mixture into the strained soup. Balance with salt and pepper to taste. Serve with garnishes of basil oil or slow-roasted corn kernels.

To make the basil oil: Blanch 1 bunch (about 4 ounces) of basil in boiling water for 10 seconds. Rinse basil in chilled water, then pat dry and blend with ¼ cup olive oil in a high-speed blender until smooth.

To make the slow-roasted corn kernels: Preheat oven to 350 degrees. Place desired amount of fresh corn kernels in shallow pan, spray with oil, and roast for 6 minutes, tossing after 3 minutes to ensure even cooking.

MEDITERRANEAN GRILLED VEGETABLE SOUP WITH ROASTED TOMATOES

4–6 SERVINGS

We recommend making this soup the morning or day before serving; it gives the flavors a chance to knit together. Also, make sure the grilled vegetables are not overcooked, as they will cook further in the soup.

2½ pounds Roma tomatoes, cut in half

4 teaspoons extra-virgin olive oil, divided

Salt and pepper to taste

⅔ cup Ravens All-Purpose Vegetable Stock (page 163) or store-bought vegan broth (optional)

1 medium eggplant, peeled and sliced into 1-inch-thick rounds

1 yellow squash, thickly sliced

1 zucchini, thickly sliced

1 red bell pepper, seeded and quartered

1 medium onion, sliced into 1-inch-thick rounds

3 tablespoons chopped roasted garlic

1½ tablespoons roughly chopped sweet basil

1½ tablespoons finely chopped Italian flat-leaf parsley

1½ teaspoons ground cumin

1½ teaspoons ground coriander

1 teaspoon sugar

⅓ teaspoon crushed fennel seed (optional)

Juice of 2 lemons (about 4 ounces)

1. Preheat oven to 450 degrees.
2. Place sliced tomatoes in a bowl with 1 teaspoon of the olive oil and a pinch of salt and pepper. Toss well and place on sheet pans, face down.
3. Roast tomatoes in oven for 20–30 minutes.
4. When tomatoes are very soft, transfer them, with their juice, to a blender; be sure not to overfill the blender. Blend until smooth, blending in separate batches if needed.
5. Strain blended tomatoes into a soup pot. If mixture is too thick, add the vegetable stock.
6. Place eggplant, squash, zucchini, red bell pepper, and onion in a bowl with remaining 3 teaspoons olive oil and salt and pepper to taste. Toss to coat well. Grill on a barbecue until just soft. If you don't have a barbecue or other grill, place on wire rack over a shallow pan in a 500-degree oven. Turn vegetables after 5 minutes and cook an additional 5 minutes.
7. Allow vegetables to cool. Chop into bite-size pieces.
8. Add roasted vegetables and remaining ingredients to tomatoes.
9. Taste and add more salt, pepper, or sugar if desired.
10. Simmer soup over medium-low heat until thoroughly heated, then serve.

ASPARAGUS SOUP WITH PISTACHIO CREAM

4–6 SERVINGS

This is a rich and delicious spring soup that blends the earthy flavor of asparagus with the special flavor of pistachio. Related to mangos, pistachios are a seed, not a true nut. Pistachios were primarily grown in the Middle East; however, the United States—led by California—is now the second largest producer in the world.

We grow hazelnuts and are adding pistachios to the crops at the inn.

---

4 quarts water

2 pounds asparagus

Salt and pepper to taste

2 tablespoons olive oil

2 medium onions, chopped

1 medium yellow-skinned potato, peeled and diced

8 cups Ravens All-Purpose Vegetable Stock (page 163) or store-bought vegan broth, divided

1 cup shelled pistachios

1 cup chopped parsley

2 tablespoons lemon juice

1. In a 6-quart pot, bring the water to a boil.
2. While water is coming to a boil, cut asparagus tips and set aside. Chop the remaining stalks into 1-inch pieces.
3. When the water has reached a rapid boil, add a pinch of salt. Put the asparagus tips in a strainer and submerge them for 2 minutes in the boiling water. Remove the tips—keep the water boiling—and rinse them immediately under cold water (this will keep them from continuing to cook). Set tips aside.
4. Put the stalks into the boiling water, reduce heat to medium, and allow stalks to simmer for 5 minutes to eliminate bitterness. Pour the water with the stalks into a colander and rinse them under cold water.
5. Heat olive oil in a 4-quart pot over medium heat; add onions, potato, and a pinch of salt and pepper. Stir occasionally, allowing the potatoes to begin to soften and the onions to turn soft and translucent but not brown (about 5 minutes).
6. Add 6 cups of the vegetable stock and the asparagus stalks to the pot. Simmer for about 20 minutes, until asparagus and potatoes have softened thoroughly.
7. Puree the asparagus, potatoes, and stock in a high-speed blender in small batches. Strain through a chinois or fine-mesh strainer to create a satiny texture.
8. In a blender, puree pistachios, parsley, remaining 2 cups vegetable stock, and lemon juice until smooth. Strain through chinois and add to the soup.
9. Serve warm, garnishing the top with the asparagus tips.

ROASTED ZUCCHINI SOUP WITH PISTACHIO CREAM AND FRESH MINT

4–6 SERVINGS

This soup calls for the ubiquitous zucchini. In late summer we are truly inundated with zucchini. Our staff and neighbors also grow this vigorous plant, and then give them away . . . to us. It is always a challenge for our chefs to use them, lots of them. This soup is one such use. The pistachio cream is a nod to California's bourgeoning pistachio plantations.

---

3 pounds zucchini, quartered

2 tablespoons olive oil, divided

½ teaspoon ground cumin

½ teaspoon ground coriander

Salt and pepper to taste

1 leek, white part only, cleaned and chopped

2 small Spanish onions, diced medium

1 tablespoon chopped fresh mint

1 tablespoon chopped fresh Italian parsley

8 cups Ravens All-Purpose Vegetable Stock (page 163) or store-bought vegan broth

Juice of 2 lemons

1 cup shelled pistachios

1. Preheat oven to 400 degrees.
2. In a large bowl, toss zucchini with 1½ tablespoons of the olive oil, cumin, coriander, and salt and pepper. Roast in the oven for 30 minutes, or until tender.
3. While the zucchini is roasting, in a sauté pan, sauté the leek and onions in the remaining ½ tablespoon olive oil over medium heat.
4. Blend zucchini, leek and onion mixture, mint, parsley, vegetable stock, and lemon juice in small batches in a high-speed blender until smooth.
5. Blend pistachios with 3 cups of the soup until smooth, and strain through a chinois to create the pistachio cream.
6. Stir the pistachio cream into the rest of the soup.
7. Balance with additional salt, pepper, and lemon juice if desired. Serve warm.

GAZPACHO

Nothing heralds the summer like gazpacho, which features an abundance of fresh ingredients such as tomatoes, cucumbers, and bell peppers. It is traditionally served cold, which can take the edge off the summer heat.

FOR THE GAZPACHO

4–5 scallions

4 large tomatoes, quartered

2 medium cucumbers, peeled and seeded

1 red bell pepper, seeded, cored, and quartered

1 small yellow onion, diced

1 jalapeño, stemmed

5 cloves garlic

1 tablespoon salt

1 teaspoon black pepper

1 quart tomato juice

¼ cup red wine vinegar

FOR THE GARNISH AND ASSEMBLY

2 tomatoes

1 small red onion

1 green bell pepper, seeded and cored

1 cucumber, seeded

For the Gazpacho

1. In a blender or food processor, blend all of the gazpacho ingredients until smooth.

For the Garnish and Assembly

1. To make the garnish, dice all of the garnish ingredients into small pieces and mix together.
2. Add garnish to soup, stir, and refrigerate for 24 hours before serving. Optionally, reserve one-fourth of the garnish to be used as a topping spooned on top of each bowl of gazpacho when served.

WATERMELON GAZPACHO

4-6 SERVINGS

Cold, refreshing, slightly spicy, and sweet—this is a great soup for awakening the palate on a late summer afternoon before a dinner of grilled vegetables and barbecued portobellos, followed by strawberry shortcake.

FOR THE GAZPACHO

1 small seedless watermelon, diced (about 7 cups), 1 cup reserved for relish (see below)

1 cup skinned, seeded, and diced tomato

1 cup peeled and seeded cucumber

½ cup minced cilantro

1 red bell pepper, seeded and roughly diced

1 red onion, diced (roughly 1 cup)

1 small jalapeño, stemmed, seeded, and chopped

2 cloves garlic

2 teaspoons salt

¼ teaspoon freshly ground black pepper

¼ cup freshly squeezed orange juice

Juice of 1 lemon

Juice of ½ lime

FOR THE WATERMELON AVOCADO RELISH AND ASSEMBLY

1 cup reserved watermelon, diced small

¼ cup diced onion

¼ cup minced cilantro

¼ cup diced cucumber

1 ripe avocado, peeled, pitted, and diced small

½ teaspoon salt

1 tablespoon orange juice

Juice of ½ lime

For the Gazpacho

1. Using a high-speed blender, blend 6 cups of the watermelon until well pureed. Set aside in large container.
2. Add all remaining gazpacho ingredients to blender and puree. Add pureed vegetable mixture to watermelon puree and chill in refrigerator.
3. Season with additional salt and pepper to taste.

For the Watermelon Avocado Relish and Assembly

1. In small mixing bowl, combine all ingredients and mix well.
2. Serve ¼-cup scoop atop each bowl of gazpacho.

POTATO LEEK SOUP WITH DRUNKEN LEEKS

4–6 SERVINGS

This is one of The Ravens' very popular soups. When it's on the menu at night, the next day there's none left for the staff "family meal."

In the days of root cellars, potato leek soups were commonly served in winter. We serve this soup year-round.

---

2 tablespoons olive oil

4–5 medium Yukon Gold or red-skinned potatoes, roughly chopped

½ cup chopped celery

⅓ cup minced parsley

3 large leeks, cleaned and thinly sliced

6 cups Ravens All-Purpose Vegetable Stock (page 163) or store-bought vegan broth

½ cup coconut cream (use the top layer of coconut cream from a can of coconut milk)

1–2 tablespoons lemon juice to taste

Salt and white pepper to taste

Drunken Leeks (see note)

Crispy Leeks (see note)

Tangy Sour Crème, for garnish (page 262)

1. Heat olive oil in a large stockpot over medium heat. Add potatoes, celery, parsley, and leeks. Cook, stirring occasionally, until vegetables are soft, 8–12 minutes.
2. Add vegetable stock, and bring mixture to a boil. Reduce heat to low, and simmer for 30–40 minutes, or until vegetables are tender.
3. Leave chunky, or blend in a high-speed blender to desired texture.
4. Lastly, add the coconut cream, and season to taste with lemon juice, salt, and white pepper.
5. Garnish with Drunken Leeks, Crispy Leeks, and Tangy Sour Crème, in that order.

To make the Drunken Leeks: Cut 2 leeks lengthwise into thin strips. In a heavy sauté pan, wilt the leek strips in 1 teaspoon olive oil over medium heat. Douse wilted leeks with 1 cup red wine and simmer for 10 minutes.

To make the Crispy Leeks: Preheat oven to 450 degrees. Slice 1 leek into ¼-inch disks and sauté in 1 teaspoon olive oil with 1 teaspoon salt. Transfer to a sheet tray and crisp up in oven for 15 minutes, or until browned.

RED PEPPER AND POTATO SOUP WITH BALSAMIC REDUCTION

4-6 SERVINGS

We have been serving this soup over many years, but most notably, on one Valentine's Day it was featured as a special dinner soup in the *Vegetarian Times*. We chose the soup for Valentine's Day because it's predominately red, the color of passion, and it contains capsicum, which improves circulation and is warming. It also contains a balsamic reduction. Casanova claimed that balsamic vinegar had aphrodisiac properties. More importantly, it is an anti-inflammatory.

FOR THE SOUP BASE

3 tablespoons olive oil

1 medium red onion, chopped

1 shallot, chopped

1 medium Yukon Gold potato, peeled and diced (approximately ½ cup)

1 medium garnet yam sweet potato, peeled and diced (approximately 1 cup)

1 tablespoon salt

1 teaspoon ground cumin

½ teaspoon ground black pepper

¼ teaspoon red pepper flakes

1 clove garlic, finely chopped

2 medium-large red bell peppers, seeded and diced

6 cups Ravens All-Purpose Vegetable Stock (page 163) or store-bought vegan broth

FOR THE BALSAMIC REDUCTION AND ASSEMBLY

1 cup balsamic vinegar

¼ cup agave syrup

For the Soup Base

1. Add oil, onion, shallot, and potatoes to a stockpot and cook over low heat until potatoes are slightly tender, about 10 minutes. (Sweet potatoes take longer.) Be careful not to overcook the other ingredients.
2. Add salt, cumin, black pepper, red pepper flakes, and garlic to the stockpot and cook for 3–5 minutes longer.
3. Add bell peppers and vegetable stock to pot and simmer for 30 minutes, until peppers and potato are completely tender.
4. Blend small batches in a high-speed blender until smooth.
5. Taste and adjust seasoning.

For the Balsamic Reduction and Assembly

1. Combine the balsamic vinegar and agave in a small saucepan and reduce over low heat until thickened and approximately half the original volume, about 15 minutes.
2. To assemble, ladle ¾–1 cup per serving of the soup into soup bowls.
3. Drizzle Balsamic Reduction on soup in a circle and draw a knife blade through the floating garnish to create a pattern. Experiment—we generally use the blade to "grab" equal long arcs of the circles (or lines), pulling them out toward the bowl's rim. Serve warm.

BROCCOLI SOUP WITH SPINACH

4-6 SERVINGS

This is the first "popular" soup of the Stanford household. It was published once as Alex's favorite in *Classy Cooking—Favorite Recipes of 4th and 5th Graders—Mendocino Grammar School*, a cookbook issued by the school. We still serve this soup on holidays when we have a chance to get together with our friends. The pureed, peeled broccoli stems give a creamy texture and flavor to this hearty soup.

1½ tablespoons olive oil

1 large onion, chopped

1 leek, both white and light green parts, cleaned and thinly sliced

1 small carrot, peeled and thinly sliced

1 stalk celery, thinly sliced

3 cloves garlic, minced

6 cups Ravens All-Purpose Vegetable Stock (page 163) or store-bought vegan broth

2 pounds (1 large bunch) broccoli, florets broken and stems peeled and sliced

½ pound (¼ head) cauliflower, chopped

1 ripe tomato

¼ cup chopped parsley

1 red bell pepper, seeded and chopped

¼ teaspoon cardamom

¼ teaspoon nutmeg

1 cup (about 4 ounces) spinach, cleaned and stemmed

Salt and pepper to taste

Tabasco sauce to taste

Juice of 1½ lemons

1. In a large stockpot, add olive oil, then cook the onion, leek, carrot, celery, and garlic over medium heat until softened, about 10 minutes.
2. Add the vegetable broth, broccoli, cauliflower, tomato, parsley, red bell pepper, cardamom, and nutmeg. Bring to a boil, then reduce heat to low. Cover and cook for 1 hour.
3. Add the spinach, salt and pepper, and Tabasco sauce to the soup.
4. Cook for 10 minutes, and then remove from the heat and puree in batches in a high-speed blender. Once blended, transfer back to the stockpot, add the lemon juice, and adjust spices according to taste. Serve hot.

ENTRÉES

Entrées are continuously changing at The Ravens. Just this afternoon, Jeff typed the menu—three new entrées, adjustments to three more, and two new soups. Not unusual. Because we use fresh ingredients, it is not possible to maintain an unchanging menu and also take advantage of our produce.

The following selection will give you a flavor of what our food is like.

INDIAN-SPICED POLENTA NAPOLEON

6–8 SERVINGS

Layers of flavors—roasted tomatoes with garlic and mint, coriander-scented zucchini, cucumber raita, and cilantro coconut relish—combine to form a fusion where Indian and Italian meet the garden. We serve this with Portobello Carpaccio—thinly sliced roasted marinated portobellos—atop a heavenly kale cashew cream sauce.

This is a great dish for any get-together. The components can be made ahead, refrigerated, and then quickly warmed, assembled, and served. It's worth the time and effort.

FOR THE POLENTA

1½ cups coarse polenta meal

4 cups water

1 teaspoon salt, divided

1 teaspoon olive oil

¼ cup diced onion

1 teaspoon minced or grated ginger

2 teaspoons minced garlic

2 teaspoons garam masala

1 teaspoon ground cumin

1 teaspoon ground coriander

3 tablespoons minced cilantro

1 teaspoon olive oil

FOR THE ROASTED TOMATOES

3 large tomatoes, sliced ¼ inch thick

¼ cup minced mint

1 teaspoon salt

½ tablespoon minced garlic

½ teaspoon pepper

1 tablespoon olive oil

FOR THE ROASTED ZUCCHINI

2 zucchini, sliced ¼ inch thick on the bias

1 tablespoon minced garlic

½ tablespoon ground coriander

½ teaspoon white pepper

1 teaspoon salt

1 tablespoon olive oil

FOR THE PORTOBELLO CARPACCIO

½ teaspoon minced garlic

Salt to taste

¼ cup white wine

¼ cup olive oil

1 teaspoon Dijon mustard

2 portobello mushrooms, stemmed

FOR THE NAPOLEON ASSEMBLY

Parchment paper

1 batch Tofu Raita (page 83)

1 batch Cilantro Mint Pesto (page 84)

1 batch Kale Sauce (page 79)

For the Polenta

1. Preheat the oven to 350 degrees.
2. Combine polenta, water, and ½ teaspoon of the salt in deep ovenproof pot or Dutch oven. Bring mixture to a boil over medium heat, stirring (or whisking) frequently.
3. Once mixture reaches boiling point, cover and place in the oven for 20 minutes, or until all water is absorbed. Alternatively, continue to cook on stove top over very low heat and whisk occasionally.

Recipe continued on next page . . .

4. In separate sauté pan, heat the oil over medium heat. Add onion, ginger, and remaining ½ teaspoon salt. Sauté over medium heat until onion is translucent, 3–5 minutes.
5. Add garlic, garam masala, cumin, and coriander. Cook for 2 minutes more, until all ingredients are incorporated. Remove from heat.
6. Add cilantro and stir to combine.
7. Fold onion spice mixture into polenta, adding olive oil to moisten.
8. Spread polenta on oiled sheet tray (½ inch thick) and refrigerate to solidify.
9. Once hardened, use ring mold to slice polenta into circles.

For the Roasted Tomatoes

1. Preheat oven to 400 degrees.
2. Combine all ingredients in large mixing bowl and toss to evenly coat tomato slices.
3. Spread out evenly on large sheet tray and roast for 20 minutes, until tomatoes are soft.

For the Roasted Zucchini

1. Preheat oven to 400 degrees.
2. Combine all ingredients in large mixing bowl and toss to evenly coat zucchini slices.
3. Spread out evenly on large sheet tray and roast for 20–25 minutes, until zucchini is tender and golden brown.

For the Portobello Carpaccio

1. Preheat oven to 550 degrees.
2. In a mixing bowl, combine all ingredients except mushrooms.
3. Once mixed thoroughly, coat each mushroom liberally with marinade and place on full sheet tray.
4. Roast gill-side up for about 10 minutes. Rotate tray and cook for another 5 minutes, or until mushrooms are tender.
5. Set aside to cool.
6. When cool, thinly slice with a sharp knife.

For the Napoleon Assembly

1. Line large sheet tray (or 2 small) with parchment paper.
2. Place polenta rounds in even lines. Dollop 1 heaping tablespoon (or more) of Tofu Raita on polenta. Top with 1 roasted tomato slice.
3. Dollop 1 tablespoon Cilantro Mint Pesto over tomato. Top with 1 slice roasted zucchini.
4. Cover and set aside in refrigerator until ready to serve.
5. Preheat oven to 350 degrees. Place sheet tray in oven and warm for 10–12 minutes before serving.
6. Serve with Kale Sauce on bottom of plate and/or drizzled over the stack.
7. Fan 3 or 4 slices of the portobello to the side of the napoleon stack.

   Note: You can also serve these with a tablespoon of Tomato Chutney (page 95) on top of the stack.

SEASONAL WILD MUSHROOM CREPE

MAKES 4-6 CREPES

Mushrooms vary seasonally, and the mushrooms in this dish follow the seasons. During the fall, we use fresh chanterelles. In January, hedgehogs replace chanterelles. After Mendocino's mushroom season has passed, we use cremini, oyster, and/or shiitake mushrooms that are available fresh throughout the year.

Although fresh porcinis, which are also known as boletes, are available after the fall's first rains, we use dried porcinis in our mushroom mixture. Fresh porcinis are amazing and are best eaten simply grilled.

The mushroom crepe can be served for all variety of occasions, including brunch.

FOR THE HERB CREPE (SEE NOTE)

16.4 ounces (about 2 cups) silken tofu

1 cup chickpea flour

2 tablespoons nutritional yeast

1½ tablespoons arrowroot powder

2 cloves garlic

1 teaspoon finely chopped chives

1 teaspoon finely chopped parsley

½ teaspoon turmeric

½ teaspoon salt

¼ teaspoon pepper

¼ cup water

2 tablespoons olive oil

FOR THE CREPE FILLING AND ASSEMBLY

2 cups dried boletes or porcini mushrooms

1 cup white wine or Ravens All-Purpose Vegetable Stock (page 163) or store-bought vegan broth

2 cups (about 1 pound) wild mushrooms, such as chanterelles or hedgehogs

2 yellow or white onions, cut into very thin half-moons

4 shallots, cut into very thin half-moons

2 tablespoons minced garlic

1 teaspoon salt

1 tablespoon white pepper

1 teaspoon green pepper

2 tablespoons olive oil

2 tablespoons minced fresh thyme

1 tablespoon dried thyme

1 bunch (about 4 ounces) chives, minced

¼ cup white wine (we use pinot gris)

1 tablespoon mirin

2 teaspoons golden balsamic vinegar

1 teaspoon ume plum vinegar

8 cups chopped raw spinach

Balsamic Reduction, for garnish (page 92)

For the Herb Crepe

1. Combine all ingredients in a high-speed blender. Blend until completely smooth. Batter will resemble a thick pancake batter.

2. Let batter rest in fridge, covered, for at least 30 minutes.

3. Heat a lightly oiled nonstick pan, griddle, or cast-iron pan over medium heat.

Recipe continued on next page . . .

4. Ladle desired amount of batter into pan (we recommend approximately ¼ cup per crepe), and gently spread batter in circular motion with ladle to thin the crepe. Crepes will be about ¼ inch thick each.

5. Brown crepe for 2½–3 minutes per side and set aside until ready to fill.

For the Crepe Filling and Assembly

1. Combine dried boletes and white wine in sauté pan over medium heat and cook until mushrooms are soft, about 5–7 minutes.

2. Allow mushrooms to cool, then remove from skillet, cut into small pieces, and set aside.

3. Using the same skillet combine wild mushrooms, onions, shallots, garlic, salt, white and green pepper, and olive oil, and sauté over medium heat until slightly brown and soft, about 10–12 minutes.

4. Add fresh and dried thyme and chives to the mushroom mixture. Deglaze pan with wine, mirin, golden balsamic vinegar, and ume plum vinegar.

5. Add spinach and stir to combine.

6. Gently combine mushroom and spinach mixture with the boletes; taste and season with salt and pepper.

7. Place a heaping ¼ cup of mushroom mixture on one half of a crepe, fold the crepe, and drizzle with Balsamic Reduction.

   Note: For thinner, crispier crepes, omit tofu, water, garlic, and nutritional yeast and replace with 1 cup soymilk. To cook, ladle ¼ cup batter into pan and quickly swirl it around to thinly coat the bottom of the pan. Flip when edges brown and begin to curl up, and cook for 1 minute on the other side.

EGGPLANT CANNELLONI

4 SERVINGS

We were asked to produce an accessible vegan recipe that could be demonstrated on television in just a few minutes. At the time, we served a grilled vegetable napoleon with tofu ricotta. For the television spot, instead of layering thinly sliced vegetables with alternating layers of tofu, we took a peeled and thinly sliced globe eggplant, stuffed it with the ricotta, rolled it up, and served it with a store-bought marinara. When we serve this dish at The Ravens Restaurant we make our own marinara and stuff the eggplant with herbed Hemp Ricotta (page 266). You can make your own marinara or use any readily available organic vegan pasta sauce.

---

1 large eggplant, peeled
(about 1 pound)

Spray oil

2 teaspoons salt

1 batch Hemp Ricotta
(page 266)

1 batch Marinara Sauce
(page 91)

Basil leaves, julienned,
for garnish

1. Preheat oven to 350 degrees.
2. Thinly slice the peeled eggplant using a mandoline.
3. Spray eggplant slices with cooking oil and dust lightly with salt.
4. Grill or broil the eggplant slices until soft, but not crisp. Set aside and let cool.
5. Once cool, fill each slice with 1–2 teaspoons of Hemp Ricotta and roll into a 1-inch-wide cylinder.
6. Place cylinders on a baking sheet and bake for 5–10 minutes, or until well heated.
7. To serve, place 6 rolls on a plate and ladle Marinara Sauce on top. Garnish with fresh julienned basil.

RAVENS REUBEN

MAKES 6–8 SANDWICHES

When Jeff was twenty he moved to New York City to intern in a multinational corporation (explaining his current penchant to live in a rural area working on the land). There he discovered Reuben's Restaurant and Delicatessen, the home of the original Reuben sandwich, and most important, Reuben's cheesecake, which Reuben's mailed anywhere in the United States. For Christmas that year he sent one to each of his family members. At Reuben's Jeff discovered two great gifts—cheesecake and a sandwich that remains an inspiration more than forty years later.

Our sandwich is made with sauerkraut, portobellos, and a vegan version of Thousand Island dressing created with our Tangy Sour Crème (page 262). To reduce the caloric load, we serve our Ravens Reuben on Flatbread (page 70), but you can use any bread you like.

FOR THE ROASTED MARINATED PORTOBELLOS

½ cup Dijon mustard

¼ cup minced garlic

1 tablespoon salt

1 teaspoon coarsely ground black pepper

2 cups dry white wine

½ cup olive oil

6 portobello mushrooms, brushed clean and stemmed

FOR THE TANGY THOUSAND ISLAND DRESSING

1 cup Tangy Sour Crème (page 262)

1 clove garlic, minced

1½ teaspoons finely diced onion

¼ cup ketchup

2 tablespoons sweet pickle relish

½ teaspoon lemon juice

1 teaspoon agave syrup

¼ teaspoon white pepper

Salt to taste

FOR THE ASSEMBLY

1 cup Ravens Vegan Cashew Cheese (page 259)

2 tablespoons soymilk

Flatbread (page 70) or any vegan bread of your choice

4 cups arugula

3 avocados, peeled, pitted, and sliced

3 tomatoes, sliced

1 (16-ounce) jar organic sauerkraut

For the Roasted Marinated Portobellos

1. Preheat oven to 425 degrees.
2. Mix all marinade ingredients except the olive oil in a mixing bowl, whisking to combine.
3. While whisking, drizzle the olive oil into the marinade.
4. Dip each mushroom cap into the marinade and place gill-side up on a sheet pan. Roast for 12–15 minutes, until tender.
5. Remove from heat and set aside.

Recipe continued on next page . . .

For the Tangy Thousand Island Dressing

1. Combine all ingredients in a bowl and refrigerate until needed.

For the Assembly

1. Grate cheese into a small saucepan, add a small amount of soymilk, and warm over low heat. Whisk to form a smooth sauce. Keep warm.
2. Warm Flatbread and portobello mushrooms on a grill or griddle. Slice mushrooms thinly.
3. Coat Flatbread with 1 tablespoon of Tangy Thousand Island Dressing.
4. Add arugula, avocado, tomato, sliced portobellos, and ¼ cup sauerkraut, and then top with melted cheese.
5. Sandwich may be place under broiler to brown, if desired.

BARBECUED PORTOBELLO OR TOFU

4–6 SERVINGS

From Kansas City, home of the famous Gates Bar-B-Q, which was "born" the same year, Jeff grew up on barbecue. Once he turned vegan he learned to barbecue tofu or tempeh. Seeking a whole-food approach, Jeff barbecued everything from zucchini to eggplant (don't bother trying) and any variety of bean burgers. He and The Ravens' team tried a whole portobello for its umami flavor and rich texture and haven't looked back since. *Note:* Smoking the portobello is not absolutely necessary. The barbecue sauce is rich and tangy and can carry the portobellos. Here we've included instructions for making either barbecue portobello or tofu.

FOR THE BARBECUED PORTOBELLO

4–6 portobello mushrooms, cleaned and de-gilled

Salt and freshly ground pepper

½ large red onion, diced small

1 tablespoon minced garlic (3 large cloves)

½ tablespoon olive oil

¾ cup apple cider vinegar

½ cup Ravens All-Purpose Vegetable Stock (page 163) or store-bought stock

2 tablespoons paprika

2 tablespoons chili powder

1 tablespoon smoked paprika

¼ cup agave syrup

Salt to taste

FOR THE BARBECUED TOFU

1 large red onion, chopped

2 tablespoons minced garlic

1 tablespoon canola oil

1½ cups apple cider vinegar

1½ cups water

¼ cup paprika

¼ cup chili powder

½ cup agave syrup

Salt and freshly ground pepper to taste

1 pound extra-firm tofu, cut into ½-inch slabs (¼ pound per serving)

FOR THE ASSEMBLY

3 cups Ravens Barbecue Sauce (page 92)

For the Barbecued Portobello

1. Season the portobellos with salt and pepper as desired, then smoke the mushrooms. There are two methods for smoking, one using a grill and one using the stove top:

   Grill Method:

   - Soak wood chips for smoking in water. Apple or alder chips work well.
   - Start a barbecue grill that allows for indirect heat and smoking, and let coals or lava become glowing without flame.
   - Throw wet wood chips onto the coals without smothering them and place mushrooms on the coolest section of the grill. Do not put over direct heat.
   - Smoke for 30–40 minutes, ensuring that the portobellos are not roasted, only smoked. Add more wet wood chips, if necessary. They should smell intensely smoky.
   - Cool mushrooms.

Stove-Top Method:

- Place soaked wood chips into a hotel pan or other large saucepan, pasta maker, or steamer with a small amount of water.
- Place a steamer or other basket with mushrooms in it over the water. Cover tightly with lid or aluminum foil.
- Place hotel pan or steamer assembly on stove top over low heat. When smoke starts coming out, set a timer for 40 minutes.
- Smell mushrooms after 40 minutes. They should have a strong smoky smell; if not, re-cover and continue smoking for an additional 10 minutes and check again.
- Once smoked, cool.

2. In a sauté pan over medium heat, sauté onion and garlic in oil until onion is translucent, about 5 minutes. Let cool. Add onion and garlic mixture and remaining ingredients to high-speed blender and blend until well incorporated.
3. Liberally cover portobellos with marinade and let marinate for at least 2 hours. To speed the process, heat mushrooms in their marinade in 350-degree oven for 10 minutes.
4. Set aside marinated mushrooms.

For the Barbecued Tofu

1. In a sauté pan over medium heat, sauté onion and garlic in oil until onion is translucent, about 5 minutes. Let cool.
2. Place onions and garlic and all remaining ingredients except tofu in a high-speed blender and blend until well incorporated.
3. Liberally cover tofu blocks in mixture and let marinate for at least 2 hours.

For the Assembly

1. Grill each portobello or piece of tofu for 2 minutes, basting with Ravens Barbecue Sauce.

   Note: Serve with mashed potatoes or Potato Salad (page 159), grilled corn on the cob, baked beans, and Jalapeño Cornbread (page 71).

BEGGAR'S PURSE

MAKES 16–18 PURSES

This is a relatively easy dish to prepare ahead of an event and is great for entertaining. These fillo dough dumplings are stuffed with mushrooms, arugula, tofu, and kombu and topped with Cashew Crème. Any combinations of mushrooms can be used, or even a single mushroom. For a healthier alternative, use whole wheat fillo. Serve with Ravens Braised Greens (page 137) and Balsamic Reduction (page 92).

FOR THE BEGGAR'S PURSES

1 shallot, diced

Pinch of salt

2 tablespoons canola oil, divided

6 oyster mushrooms, finely chopped

4 shiitake mushrooms, finely chopped

4 cremini mushrooms, finely chopped

2 tablespoons kombu, finely ground in food processor

3 cloves garlic, minced

1 tablespoon mirin

1 cup crumbled tofu

1 cup arugula

1 teaspoon red pepper flakes

1 teaspoon lemon juice

FOR THE CASHEW CRÈME AND ASSEMBLY

1 cup cashews, soaked for 20–30 minutes and drained

1 tablespoon miso paste

1 teaspoon minced green pepper

1 teaspoon salt

1 teaspoon nutritional yeast

Juice of 1 lemon

1 (16-ounce) package whole wheat fillo, thawed and cut into 8-inch squares

Spray oil

For the Beggar's Purses

1. In a sauté pan over medium heat, sauté shallot with a pinch of salt in 1 tablespoon of the canola oil for five minutes.
2. Add all mushrooms, kombu, and garlic to the shallots. Deglaze pan with mirin.
3. In separate pan over medium heat, sauté tofu in the remaining 1 tablespoon canola oil with a pinch of salt for 10 minutes. When tofu is browned, add to mushroom mixture.
4. Lastly, fold in arugula, red pepper flakes, and lemon juice.
5. Set aside to cool.

For the Cashew Crème and Assembly

1. Preheat oven to 350 degrees.
2. Blend the cashews, miso, green pepper, salt, nutritional yeast, and lemon juice in a high-speed blender or food processor until combined. Mixture should be thick.
3. In large muffin tin, layer six 8 x 8-inch squares of whole wheat fillo dough, spraying each layer with a fine mist of oil.
4. On each square of fillo, place 1 tablespoon of Cashew Crème and then 2 tablespoons of mushroom mixture.
5. Spray with mist of oil and gently fold and twist dough of each square together. The dough should look like a small purse.
6. Bake for 15–20 minutes, or until golden brown.

Note: Once assembled these purses can be frozen before baking and served at a later date. Thaw before baking and follow the same baking instructions.

BLACK PEPPER FETTUCCINE WITH CHARDONNAY SAUCE AND GRILLED ASPARAGUS

4 SERVINGS

This pasta, like many pasta dishes, is a "crossover" dish, meaning that it's appealing to non-vegans and vegans alike. And a crossover dish must in itself be intriguing.

This recipe was featured in *Vegetarian Times* as a main course for a romantic Valentine's dinner. The ingredients, as those in other dishes in this book, enhance health: Pepper is an anti-inflammatory. Kudzu, considered a weed in the South, has been found to reduce blood pressure and significantly reduce alcohol ingestion. The peppery pasta goes well with asparagus, which, because of its shape, makes the dish a great Valentine's entrée. A whole food, asparagus is a rich source of folate and contains the glutathione that protects cells from toxins. *Note: You may substitute ready-made fettuccini.*

FOR THE PASTA

1 cup all-purpose flour

1 cup semolina

1 tablespoon kudzu root powder (substitute arrowroot if desired)

1 tablespoon coarsely ground black pepper

¾ tablespoon salt

½ cup olive oil

1½ cups warm water

FOR THE CHARDONNAY CREAM SAUCE

1 cup chardonnay

1 cup raw cashews

1 cup water

1 tablespoon nutritional yeast

1½ teaspoons freshly cracked pepper

Salt to taste

1 tablespoon freshly squeezed lemon juice

FOR THE WILTED SPINACH

2 cups baby spinach

½ cup water or Ravens All-Purpose Vegetable Stock (page 163) or store-bought vegan broth

FOR THE ASPARAGUS

10 asparagus spears

Spray oil

FOR THE ASSEMBLY

3–5 thinly sliced red bell pepper strips, for garnish

For the Pasta

1. In a large mixing bowl, combine flour, semolina, kudzu root powder, black pepper, salt, olive oil, and warm water.
2. Mix for approximately 7–10 minutes, until dough consistency is reached.
3. On a floured surface, roll the dough into a log and slice into 2–3-inch sections to make the dough more manageable. Roll the sections out with a roller or pasta maker to approximately ¹⁄₁₆ inch thickness. Cut again into ¼-inch strips to form the fettuccini (see note). Do not pile the fettuccini. The strips should remain separated until cooked or stored.

4. If storing, dry strips by hanging from a pasta rack or by laying across a wire rack for a couple of hours. Divide the fettuccini into two equal amounts, and place each half loosely into a 1-gallon freezer bag and freeze.

For the Chardonnay Cream Sauce

1. In small saucepan, reduce chardonnay over high heat until only approximately ¾ cup liquid remains.
2. In a high-speed blender, combine cashews and water, and blend until smooth.
3. Strain cashew mixture through cheesecloth, and add to reduced chardonnay. While stirring, add nutritional yeast, cracked pepper, salt, and lemon juice.
4. Cook over medium heat for approximately 10 minutes.

For the Wilted Spinach

1. In sauté pan, add spinach to water and wilt over low heat.

For the Asparagus

1. Lightly spray asparagus with oil and grill until grill marks show on the spears. Turn once to cook the other side. Cooking time should take total of about 3 minutes. Alternatively, you can place the asparagus in a sauté pan and cook until they're bright green (about 3–4 minutes). Turn, then cook other side for another 3–4 minutes, for a total 7 minutes cooking time.
2. Cut cooked asparagus into approximately 2-inch pieces.

For the Assembly

1. Cook the pasta in boiling water for 5 minutes or until al dente.
2. Toss cooked pasta in chardonnay sauce to lightly coat, and place each serving in an individual pasta bowl.
3. Top each bowl of pasta with approximately one-fourth of the wilted spinach, and cross 2 asparagus spears over the spinach.
4. Ladle a tablespoon of the chardonnay sauce over the spears and spinach greens.
5. Place a few red pepper strips atop the chardonnay sauce and serve warm.

Note: We use a pasta maker rather than cutting up the fettuccini by hand.

VEGETABLE NAPOLEON

4-6 SERVINGS; 3-4 PER PERSON

Primarily a summer dish, this Vegetable Napoleon offers a range of flavors, colors, and textures, from a yielding smoothness to a walnut crunch. Feel free to use any seasonal vegetables you have on hand and have fun.

FOR THE ZUCCHINI

1 tablespoon fresh thyme

2 tablespoons chopped fresh oregano or 1 tablespoon dried oregano

1 tablespoon lemon zest

1 clove garlic, minced

1 teaspoon salt

½ teaspoon black pepper

3 tablespoons olive oil

3 zucchini, peeled and sliced into ½-inch disks

FOR THE SUMMER ROASTED TOMATO

1 clove garlic, minced

4 fresh basil leaves, thinly sliced into strips

½ teaspoon salt

½ teaspoon pepper

2 tablespoons olive oil

3 tomatoes, sliced into ½-inch disks

½ cup walnuts

FOR THE ASSEMBLY

½ cup Pumpkin Seed, Arugula, and Mint Pesto (page 88)

1 batch Tofu Ricotta (page 261)

Baby arugula, for garnish

Juice of 1 lemon

2 tablespoons olive oil

Salt to taste

Balsamic Reduction, for garnish (page 92; optional)

For the Zucchini

1. Preheat oven to 350 degrees.
2. Mix thyme, oregano, lemon zest, garlic, salt, black pepper, and olive oil in a large bowl.
3. Toss zucchini in oil mixture until disks are evenly coated.
4. Lay pieces on oiled sheet tray and bake for 15–20 minutes, or until zucchini are tender and golden brown.
5. Let cool before handling.

For the Summer Roasted Tomato

1. Preheat oven to 350 degrees.
2. Mix garlic, basil, salt, pepper, and olive oil in a large bowl.
3. Toss tomatoes in the mixture until evenly coated.
4. Lay out slices on a well-oiled sheet tray and bake for 10–15 minutes, or until tender.
5. While the tomatoes are roasting, evenly spread walnuts on a baking sheet and toast for 10 minutes, stirring occasionally for even toasting.
6. Let cool before handling.

For the Assembly

1. Lay out 1 piece of zucchini and spread a layer (about 1 tablespoon) of pesto on top.
2. Spread a layer of Tofu Ricotta (about 1 tablespoon) on top of the pesto, and then top with 1 slice of tomato.
3. To garnish, toss baby arugula with small amount of lemon juice, olive oil, and salt. Place mixture on top of the tomato. Garnish with extra ricotta, toasted walnuts, and Balsamic Reduction.

ALMOND HAZELNUT-ENCRUSTED TEMPEH

4–6 SERVINGS

Whole food! Tempeh is a fermented soy product, and as those of you who have cooked it before will know, it sometimes retains the taste of the culture used for fermentation. In this recipe, the marinade helps wash away the taste of the culture. The almonds and hazelnuts provide a crunchy crust. If there is leftover encrusted tempeh from the dinner preparation, we put it out for our staff, who eat it like kids eating fish sticks.

This dish is perfect to use as the base for any holiday entrée; serve with mashed potatoes, mushroom gravy, and a fruit sauce: cranberry—what else?

FOR THE MARINATED TEMPEH

1 tablespoon sliced ginger

2 cloves garlic, sliced

3 cups water

¼ cup gluten-free tamari

1 (6.5-ounce) package tempeh, sliced ½ inch thick on the bias

FOR THE FLAX "EGG" WASH

2 tablespoons ground flaxseeds

½ cup warm water

FOR THE ALMOND HAZELNUT CRUST AND ASSEMBLY

½ cup raw almonds

½ cup hazelnuts

¼ teaspoon salt

Freshly ground black pepper

Spray oil or 2 tablespoons olive oil

For the Marinated Tempeh

1. Combine ginger, garlic, water, and tamari in a saucepan and add the sliced tempeh. Cook until tempeh his heated through, about 10–15 minutes.
2. Drain tempeh from cooking liquid, set aside, and let cool.

For the Flax "Egg" Wash

1. In large mixing bowl, combine flaxseeds and warm water and whisk until thickened. More water may be added as necessary; mixture should resemble thick pancake batter.

For the Almond Hazelnut Crust and Assembly

1. In food processor, combine almonds and hazelnuts and process until coarse, sandlike consistency is achieved.
2. Add salt and pepper and process for a moment longer until well incorporated.
3. Place in a small mixing bowl and set aside.
4. Preheat oven to 350 degrees.
5. Dip each slice of tempeh into the flax wash and immediately dredge in the almond and hazelnut mixture until the tempeh is well coated.
6. Spray a large baking sheet with cooking spray, then set tempeh slices on it.
7. Bake for 20–30 minutes, until golden brown and crisp.
8. Alternatively, place 2 tablespoons olive oil in a sauté pan, or oil a griddle and heat to medium heat. Place each piece of tempeh on the pan or griddle and cook until golden brown on each side (5–7 minutes per side).

RAVENS SPICY PEANUT CURRY SEA PALM

4-6 SERVINGS

Years ago the owners of the Mendocino Sea Vegetable Company gave us dried sea palm and said, "See what you can do with this." Sea palm is a nutritious brown seaweed, full of vitamins A and C, calcium, and much more; it's also harvested on our eco-friendly coast of Mendocino. Here, the rivers are short and there are no cities or major agricultural operations along their banks.

We created our Ravens Sea Palm Strudel (page 212) and this incredible Spicy Peanut Curry Sea Palm. In the Spicy Peanut Curry Sea Palm, sea palm serves as a noodle rather than a filling.

Ravens Spicy Peanut Curry Sea Palm is a multipart dish—but it's worth the work. Prepare the sea palm the day before serving, and also make the vegetables and brown rice ahead of time; make the sauce the same day, and follow by braising the vegetables.

Find sea palm at Whole Foods Market or similar stores. Sea palm can also be found online.

FOR THE SEA PALM NOODLES

3 ounces (about 2 cups) dried sea palm

2 cups water

3 tablespoons minced garlic

2 tablespoons grated ginger

¼ teaspoon red pepper flakes (optional)

¼ cup tamari

2 tablespoons brown rice syrup

2 tablespoons brown rice vinegar

1 teaspoon toasted sesame oil

FOR THE BRAISED SEASONAL VEGETABLES

½ cup Ravens All-Purpose Vegetable Stock (page 163) or store-bought vegan broth

1 teaspoon tamari

¼ cup coarsely chopped yellow onion

½ cup broccoli florets or chopped broccolini

½ cup cauliflower florets

1 red bell pepper, seeded and julienned

1 yellow bell pepper, seeded and julienned

1 cup half-moon-sliced yellow squash

1 baby eggplant, cut into chunks

2 cups sliced bok choy

FOR THE SPICY PEANUT CURRY SAUCE

1 cup organic creamy peanut butter

¼ cup diced red onion

1 tablespoon ground coriander

1 tablespoon turmeric

1 tablespoon grated fresh ginger

2 teaspoons ground cumin

1 jalapeño pepper, seeded

2 cloves garlic

¼ teaspoon red pepper flakes

Zest and juice of 2 limes

1 (13.5-ounce) can organic coconut milk

¼ cup agave syrup

Salt and pepper to taste

FOR THE ASSEMBLY

2 cups cooked brown rice

½ cup roasted peanuts

Lime wedges

Recipe continued on next page . . .

For the Sea Palm Noodles

1. Cover dried sea palm with the water and soak overnight.
2. Drain sea palm and place in large pot.
3. Cover sea palm with remaining ingredients and simmer 20–30 minutes, until sea palm is tender like the texture of a noodle. Do not overcook, or sea palm will be too soft.

For the Braised Seasonal Vegetables

1. Place a wok over medium-high heat and add broth and tamari.
2. Quickly toss in onion followed by other vegetables.
3. Continue tossing vegetables and cook only 3–5 minutes. Vegetables should remain firm.
4. Set aside.

For the Spicy Peanut Curry Sauce

1. In a high-speed blender or food processor, combine all ingredients except salt and pepper, and blend until smooth and well mixed. Water may be added to help blend mixture to a creamy texture. If using a food processor, blend longer, and note that the mixture may not get completely smooth.
2. Add salt and pepper to taste.
3. Set aside.

For the Assembly

1. Place ½–¾ cup brown rice in the bottom of a pasta bowl.
2. Add approximately ½ cup of sea palm noodles on top of rice.
3. Drizzle noodles and rice with Spicy Peanut Curry Sauce.
4. Top with ½ cup braised vegetables and drizzle lightly with additional sauce.
5. Garnish with roasted peanuts and lime wedges.

PAELLA

While living in Spain, Jeff discovered paella. Returning to the United States, he re-created traditional paella for his family. After becoming vegan and opening The Ravens, he found that it was a dish that intimidated seasoned chefs, most of whom were not vegan, not even vegetarian. They could not conceive of paella without pork and seafood.

Paella is a dish based on leftovers. Jeff's Spanish family served it almost weekly. Their base flavor was saffron and bacon fat. In this version, the saffron remains and Shiitake Bacon replaces the pork bacon and sausage.

Give this paella a try; it's sure to please any crowd. And don't leave out the Shiitake Bacon! We find that using it really brings this dish together.

---

2 cups short-grain brown rice

2 tablespoons sunflower oil, divided

Pinch of salt

4 cloves garlic, minced

1 medium yellow onion, diced

2 dried shiitake mushrooms, rehydrated and chopped, reserving the liquid

1½ teaspoons saffron

1 teaspoon paprika

½ teaspoon white pepper

½ teaspoon green pepper

1 carrot, diced

1 red bell pepper, seeded and diced

1 green bell pepper, seeded and diced

1 bunch (about 4 ounces) chives, diced

1 shallot, diced

2 tomatoes, diced

1 zucchini, diced

1 (3.5-ounce) jar capers, drained

2 tablespoons mirin

1 strip dried kombu

3 shiitake mushrooms, finely chopped

2 bay leaves

4–6 cups Ravens All-Purpose Vegetable Stock (page 163) or store-bought vegan broth

½ cup white wine

½ cup frozen green peas

1 bunch (about 4 ounces) parsley, chopped

1 tablespoon fresh lemon juice (preferably Meyer lemon)

1 cup Shiitake Bacon, for garnish (page 265)

Assorted grilled vegetables (zucchini, red/green bell pepper, carrots), cooked al dente, for garnish

---

1. In large pot, combine rice and 1 tablespoon of the sunflower oil with the salt. Lightly sauté the rice over medium heat, stirring often with a large wooden spoon, until light brown and fragrant, about 10 minutes. Be mindful not to burn. Remove from heat.

2. While the rice is cooking, add remaining 1 tablespoon sunflower oil to a large sauté pan and lightly sauté the garlic, onion, and rehydrated shiitake mushrooms with the saffron, paprika, and white and green pepper for about 5 minutes, or until the mixture becomes fragrant and the onions start to become translucent. Add

Recipe continued on next page . . .

the carrot, bell peppers, chives, shallot, tomatoes, zucchini, and capers and continue cooking another 5 minutes to combine all the flavors. Add mirin to deglaze pan, and transfer the vegetable mixture to the large pot with toasted rice.

3. Add reserved shiitake stock, kombu, shiitake mushrooms, and bay leaves to the rice. Add vegetable stock (pour in just enough stock to cover the rice). Simmer for 45–50 minutes with the pot covered. Check often to make sure rice is not sticking to bottom of the pan. If the rice does start to stick, add more stock.

4. After the rice has cooked about 50 minutes, remove the kombu and add the white wine and continue cooking for another 8–10 minutes. Add more stock if necessary to prevent the rice from adhering to the pan.

5. Add frozen peas, parsley, and lemon juice at the end of the cooking process, and simmer for an additional 5 minutes.

6. Pour cooked rice mixture into a paella pan or serving dish. Season with salt and pepper.

7. Garnish with Shiitake Bacon and grilled vegetables and serve.

RAVENS SEA PALM STRUDEL

4 SERVINGS

If The Ravens has a signature dish, the Sea Palm Strudel is it. Sea palm grows just off our coast, has a rich flavor, and is not slimy like some seaweed. Resa Soloway, one of our interns, worked on this creation, which began as a simple appetizer. Over the years, we have made small changes and today it is one of our most beloved entrées.

The strudel is rolled in very thin sheets of dough that are variously spelled phyllo, filo, or fillo. We use a whole wheat product that uses the variant *fillo* in its name and we have chosen to use this spelling throughout *Dining at The Ravens*. *Fillo* means leaf in Greek.

We serve Ravens Sea Palm Strudel with a stir-fry of fresh vegetables from our garden, organic cashews, and two special sauces, Ume Plum Sauce (below), and Wasabi Sauce (page 90).

FOR THE SEA PALM STRUDEL

4 ounces sea palm, soaked for 5 minutes in enough warm water to cover

4 cups water

1 cup brown rice syrup

6 tablespoons tamari

1 tablespoon grated fresh ginger

1 onion, thinly sliced

2 carrots, julienned

2 tablespoons water or Ravens All-Purpose Vegetable Stock (page 163) or store-bought vegan broth

1 tablespoon sesame oil

1 (16-ounce) package whole wheat fillo dough (we use Fillo Factory Organic Whole Wheat Fillo Dough)

Spray oil or ¼ cup olive oil

2 tablespoons black sesame seeds

FOR THE UME PLUM SAUCE

½ (10-ounce) bag frozen raspberries

3½ tablespoons umeboshi plum paste

Juice of 1 lime

1 cup apple juice

2 tablespoons arrowroot powder

FOR THE ASIAN STIR-FRY

1 tablespoon sunflower oil

1 medium white onion, chopped

1 clove garlic, minced

1 cup chopped broccoli

1 cup chopped cauliflower

½ cup coarsely chopped red or green pepper

½ cup chopped red or green cabbage

1 large carrot, cut into ⅛-inch slices

Pinch of red pepper flakes

½ cup Ravens All-Purpose Vegetable Stock (page 163) or store-bought vegan broth

¼ cup cashews

FOR THE ASSEMBLY

1 batch Wasabi Sauce (page 90)

For the Sea Palm Strudel

1. Preheat oven to 450 degrees.
2. In a large saucepan, combine drained sea palm, water, brown rice syrup, and tamari.

Recipe continued on next page . . .

3. Over medium heat, bring mixture to a slow boil. Lower heat and simmer until the liquid turns to syrup, about 15 minutes.

4. Add ginger, remove the saucepan from the heat, and allow to cool.

5. In a medium saucepan, braise onion and carrots in the stock and sesame oil. Lower heat to low and allow the onions and carrots to soften, about 15 minutes. Set aside to cool.

6. To assemble, lay down 1 sheet of fillo dough and brush or spray lightly with olive oil. Place a second sheet on top of the first and brush with oil again. Repeat with a third layer. Sprinkle black sesame seeds over the whole third sheet. Layer 2 more sheets of fillo, brushing each with oil (for total of 5 layers). Sprinkle black sesame seeds on the top layer.

7. Spread a 3-inch wide strip of the cooled sea palm mixture evenly across the fillo sheets, 2 inches from the bottom. Lift the bottom edge up and over the sea palm mixture, rolling and securing the mixture. Then place a 3-inch-wide strip of the cooled carrot and onion mixture evenly across the top of the secured sea palm mixture. Roll the sea palm up and over the carrot mixture, securing the mixture. Continue to gently roll up. Place, seam-side down, onto a greased baking sheet.

8. Bake for 15–20 minutes, or until golden brown and heated through. Allow to rest for 5–10 minutes.

For the Ume Plum Sauce

1. In a small saucepan, combine the raspberries, plum paste, and lime juice. Add apple juice, using only enough to cover the mixture. Bring to a boil over medium heat.

2. In a small bowl, combine the arrowroot with a ½ teaspoon water to make a milky paste. Add additional water if necessary.

3. Carefully add the arrowroot mixture to the boiling raspberry mixture. Mix well and remove from heat.

4. Set sauce aside until ready for assembly or store in refrigerator for up to 5 days.

For the Asian Stir-Fry

1. In a large sauté pan, heat sunflower oil and add onion and garlic.

2. Sauté for 2 minutes over medium heat, then add remaining vegetables and red pepper flakes, tossing occasionally.

3. When the broccoli begins to brighten, pour in the vegetable stock, toss vegetables to coat, reduce heat to low, and cover pan to steam the vegetables.

4. Toss vegetables again after 5 minutes, and replenish vegetable stock if needed to coat vegetables. Continue to cook until just tender, another 5 minutes.

5. Just before serving, toss cashews into the vegetables.

For the Assembly

1. Using a serrated knife, slice the strudel into 2-inch pieces and place 3 on one side of each of 4 plates.

2. Place about ½ cup of stir-fry in front of strudel pieces; half the plate should now be filled with strudel and stir-fry.

3. Carefully spread 2 tablespoons of Ume Plum Sauce on the other side of the plate.

4. Using a squirt bottle or a pastry bag with a fine tip (you can also use a zip-top bag with the corner cut to make a fine tip), squeeze out a thin zigzag line of the Wasabi Sauce onto the plum sauce, so that you have many short green lines.

5. Starting at the top on the far side of the sauce, drag a toothpick through the plum sauce and green lines. This will create a scalloped look. Repeat every 2 inches, switching direction each new line.

SUN-DRIED TOMATO POLENTA WITH FORAGED MUSHROOMS AND ARUGULA

4–6 SERVINGS

A substantial and amazing winter entrée, this recipe begins with a taste of summer past: sun-dried tomatoes, corn, and polenta. We place this atop our winter-grown arugula that has been wilted, and cover it all with lightly sautéed wild mushrooms. We add our Cashew Morel Cream, and a sprinkling of Shiitake Bacon and serve with roasted Brussels sprouts. This can be made ahead, with the exception of the arugula, and assembled for entertaining.

FOR THE SUN-DRIED TOMATO POLENTA

¾ cup sun-dried tomatoes

2 cups warm water

3 tablespoons olive oil, divided

¾ cup diced red onion

¼ cup diced shallot

2 cloves garlic, minced

¼ teaspoon red pepper flakes (optional)

1½ cups coarse polenta (see note)

3 cups water or Ravens All-Purpose Vegetable Stock (page 163) or store-bought vegan broth

1 teaspoon salt

¼ teaspoon pepper

¼ cup thinly bias-sliced scallion

1 tablespoon minced fresh thyme

1 tablespoon minced fresh oregano

1 tablespoon chiffonade fresh basil

Parchment paper

FOR THE WILTED ARUGULA

1 tablespoon olive oil

4 cups arugula

1 clove garlic, minced

Pinch of red pepper flakes (optional)

½ teaspoon salt

¼ teaspoon pepper

FOR THE FORAGED MUSHROOMS

1 tablespoon olive oil

4 cups wild, locally foraged mushrooms, cleaned and roughly chopped (e.g., chanterelles, oysters, porcinis, or preferred wild mushrooms)

1 tablespoon minced fresh thyme

1 teaspoon salt

½ teaspoon black pepper

FOR THE ROASTED BRUSSELS SPROUTS

2 pounds Brussels sprouts, bases trimmed (if sprout is particularly large, cut through the base toward the top approximately ½ inch)

3 tablespoons olive oil

½ teaspoon salt

¼ teaspoon white pepper

FOR THE ASSEMBLY

1½ cups Cashew Morel Cream (page 86)

1 batch Shiitake Bacon, for garnish (page 265)

For the Sun-Dried Tomato Polenta

1. Soak sun-dried tomatoes in water for about 30 minutes, or until rehydrated. Reserve soaking liquid.

2. In a large sauté pan, heat 2 tablespoons of the olive oil and cook onion and shallots over medium-low heat until slightly translucent. Add garlic and red pepper flakes and cook for a minute longer.

Recipe continued on next page . . .

3. Add polenta and coat the grains well with the oil and onion mixture. Add water and raise the heat. Using a whisk, mix thoroughly until polenta starts to thicken. Add salt and pepper (if using stock, limit the amount of salt you use—many stocks are high in sodium).
4. Bring to boil. Adjust heat to low and stir frequently. Cook polenta for 20–30 minutes, until the grains are tender and well cooked (some cooking times may vary depending on the size of the grain). If more liquid is required to prevent the mixture from sticking to the pan, add reserved sun-dried tomato soaking water little by little (1–2 tablespoons at a time).
5. Once polenta is cooked, fold in scallions, thyme, oregano, basil and remaining 1 tablespoon olive oil. Season further with salt and pepper to taste.
6. Spread polenta mixture out on a baking sheet that has been lined with parchment paper, pressing with an oiled rubber spatula until polenta is ½ inch thick.
7. Set aside and chill in refrigerator.
8. Cut polenta into wedges and reheat in oiled sauté pan until polenta is crispy and golden on each side and heated thoroughly, about 5 minutes.

For the Wilted Arugula

1. In large sauté pan, heat oil over medium-low heat. Add arugula and let wilt and crisp slightly.
2. Add garlic and red pepper flakes and sauté for a moment longer until garlic is cooked, then lower heat to prevent garlic from burning.
3. Season with salt and pepper.

For the Foraged Mushrooms

1. Heat oil in large sauté pan and cook mushrooms over medium heat until they are well cooked and slightly crispy, about 20 minutes. Do not crowd mushrooms.
2. Add thyme, salt, and pepper at the very end of cooking.

For the Roasted Brussels Sprouts

1. Preheat oven to 400 degrees.
2. Place all ingredients in a bowl, tossing to coat the Brussels sprouts.
3. Spread Brussels sprouts in a single layer across a sheet pan and bake for 30 minutes, or until golden and tender. Turn sprouts after first 15 minutes.

For the Assembly

1. For each serving, spoon 2 tablespoons of Cashew Morel Cream in the center of the plate and spread with the bottom of the spoon followed by approximately ½ cup wilted arugula. The arugula should be in the shape of a mound.
2. Place 2 pieces of polenta over the arugula.
3. Top dish with sautéed mushrooms, roasted Brussels sprouts, and Shiitake Bacon.

Polenta Note: Instant polenta can be used; adjust cooking times according to package directions.

FORBIDDEN RISOTTO WITH SUNCHOKE LEMON CREAM

4-6 SERVINGS

Sunchokes, also known as Jerusalem artichokes, are tubers from giant sunflower plants whose flowers are tiny. Providing high-quality complex carbohydrates, substantial fiber, and phytonutrients, sunchokes are also known in Mendocino as the below-ground zucchini. A nutritionally valuable crop, sunchokes also contribute significant carbon to recharge soils through aerobic composting.

In this recipe we use black "forbidden" rice, once thought to be reserved only for the Chinese emperor and his family. Combined with sunchokes, this dish is healthy and delicious!

FOR THE SUNCHOKE LEMON CREAM

1 tablespoon olive oil

½ cup diced onion

1 shallot, minced

1 clove garlic, minced

2 cups cleaned, peeled, cooked, and cubed sunchoke

½ cup water

1½ teaspoons salt

¼ teaspoon pepper

Zest and juice of 1 lemon

1 tablespoon orange juice

FOR THE RISOTTO AND ASSEMBLY

½ cup black rice (also called purple rice)

1¼ cups water

2 teaspoons olive oil

½ cup diced onion

½ cup diced celery

1 shallot, minced

½ teaspoon salt

1 cup short-grain brown rice

2 cups Ravens All-Purpose Vegetable Stock (page 163) or store-bought vegan broth (low sodium or sodium free)

For the Sunchoke Lemon Cream

1. In medium sauté pan, combine olive oil, onion, shallot, and garlic. Cook over low heat until onion is translucent, about 5 minutes.
2. Add sunchokes and water. Cook until heated and flavors are incorporated. Let cool.
3. Transfer mixture to high-speed blender or food processor and add salt, pepper, lemon zest and juice, and orange juice. Blend until all ingredients are completely smooth.

For the Risotto and Assembly

1. In small saucepan, combine black rice and water. Bring to a boil over high heat. Reduce heat to low, cover pan, and simmer for 30 minutes, or until water is absorbed. Remove from heat and let stand for 5–10 minutes before uncovering. Set aside.
2. In a separate medium saucepan, combine olive oil, onion, celery, shallot, and salt. Cook over medium heat until onion is translucent, about 5 minutes.
3. Add short-grain brown rice to saucepan and mix with the onion and celery. Coat grains with mixture and toast for a minute longer.
4. Heat vegetable stock in a separate pot.
5. Add hot stock to rice mixture and bring to boil. Reduce heat to low, cover pot, and simmer 40–50 minutes. Remove from heat and let stand 10 minutes before removing lid.
6. In large bowl or pot, combine black rice with short-grain brown rice and pour in Sunchoke Lemon Cream. Mix well until all grains are well coated.
7. Season with additional salt and pepper to taste, and serve hot.

RAW LASAGNA

4-6 SERVINGS

The Mendocino coast is home to Cherie Soria and Dan Ladermann's Living Light Culinary Institute, "the world's premier raw vegan culinary school," and "the birthplace of gourmet raw vegan cuisine." Their students often come to The Ravens, and we created this dish for them (we've learned, however, that they often prefer cooked food!). This lasagna is easy and will satisfy friends who prefer raw or live foods in all their natural beauty!

FOR THE RAW CASHEW CREAM "CHEESE"

1 cup raw cashews, soaked 12 hours or overnight and drained

1 tablespoon raw agave syrup

1 tablespoon raw yellow miso

Pinch of salt

1–1½ cups water

FOR THE BASIL PESTO

¼ cup raw sunflower seeds, soaked in water for 1–2 hours and drained

2 bunches (about 8 ounces) fresh basil

2 tablespoons raw yellow miso

1 tablespoon nutritional yeast

1 teaspoon minced garlic

Salt and pepper to taste

2 tablespoons olive oil

FOR THE ASSEMBLY

3 zucchinis, thinly sliced (see note)

3 medium heirloom tomatoes, thinly sliced (see note)

Fresh basil, for garnish (optional)

¼ cup Balsamic Reduction (page 92), for drizzling (optional; not technically raw)

For the Raw Cashew Cream "Cheese"

1. Place cashews in a food processor and process until they reach a consistency similar to ricotta.

2. Add the remaining ingredients and process until smooth. If the nuts clump add enough water to maintain a ricotta consistency.

3. If you own a dehydrator, place the mixture in a shallow pan and dehydrate at 105 degrees for 4 hours.

4. To remove excess water without a dehydrator, remove cashew mixture from food processor and spread evenly on a shallow baking sheet. Place in a warm area of your kitchen, preferably with moving air. If available, direct a fan on its gentlest setting over the cashew mixture. Let "dehydrate" for 4 hours.

5. Using a fine-mesh sieve and/or cheesecloth, press as much water as possible out of the cashew mixture.

6. If the cashew mixture is not creamy, reprocess until creamy in a food processor. Adjust sweetness and salt if desired.

For the Basil Pesto

1. Place all ingredients in food processor and blend until smooth, adding more oil if desired to achieve a smoother texture.

For the Assembly

1. Gently fold Basil Pesto into Raw Cashew Cream "Cheese."

2. Create lasagna stacks by layering the following in order: zucchini slice, basil cashew mixture, zucchini slice, tomato slice, zucchini slice.

3. Garnish with fresh basil and Balsamic Reduction.

Zucchini and Tomato Note: For best results, create very thin slices using a mandoline. Optional vegetable additions we often use are carrot and red onion, sliced on the bias.

CHANTERELLE AND FALL VEGETABLE-STUFFED PORTOBELLO

Chanterelles are wonderful. In this dish, chanterelle earthiness is balanced by roasted fall vegetables all served in portobello caps smeared with our Parsley Kale Pesto. This robust dish can be served on its own or with a side of grains such as quinoa or forbidden rice, one of our favorites for its nutty flavor and deep purple color.

FOR THE MARINATED PORTOBELLOS

3 tablespoons whole-grain mustard

1 tablespoon chopped fresh sage

1 tablespoon salt

½ tablespoon minced fresh rosemary

5 cloves garlic, minced

1 teaspoon pepper

½ cup white wine

¼ cup olive oil

2 tablespoons golden balsamic vinegar or white wine vinegar

2 tablespoons vegan Worcestershire sauce (optional)

4-6 portobello mushrooms, stems and gills removed

Spray oil

FOR THE HARVEST STUFFING

1½ cups peeled and diced sweet potato

1½ cups peeled and diced beets

1½ cups peeled, seeded, and diced butternut squash

3 tablespoons sunflower oil, divided

1 tablespoon minced fresh thyme

½ tablespoon minced fresh rosemary

1 teaspoon salt

½ teaspoon pepper

2 cups (about 1 pound) chanterelle mushrooms (or other wild mushroom), cleaned and sliced ¼ inch thick

FOR THE KALE PARSLEY PESTO

1 bunch kale, stemmed (about 4 cups tightly packed)

1 bunch parsley, stemmed (about 2 cups tightly packed)

⅓ cup pumpkin seeds, soaked for 20–30 minutes and drained

2 cloves garlic

¾ teaspoon salt

½ teaspoon pepper

⅓ cup olive oil

For the Marinated Portobellos

1. Preheat oven to 350 degrees.
2. Combine all ingredients except the portobellos and spray oil in a large mixing bowl. Whisk ingredients together until well incorporated and emulsified.
3. Dip each portobello into the marinade mixture and place gill-side up on a sheet tray or shallow pan that has been lightly sprayed with oil.
4. Bake for 20–30 minutes until mushrooms are softened and begin to fill with juice.
5. Set aside and let cool slightly before stuffing.

Recipe continued on next page . . .

For the Harvest Stuffing

1. Preheat oven to 350 degrees.
2. Combine sweet potatoes, beets, and butternut squash in a large bowl. Toss with 2 tablespoons of the oil, spread on a sheet tray, and roast for 25–35 minutes, until golden brown and tender.
3. Remove from oven and sprinkle with fresh herbs, salt, and pepper. Toss gently to incorporate flavors.
4. In sauté pan, combine mushrooms and remaining 1 tablespoon oil and cook over medium heat until mushrooms are tender and golden brown, about 7 minutes.
5. Gently toss cooked mushrooms with roasted vegetables and set aside.

For the Kale Parsley Pesto

1. Steam or blanch kale until tender. Drain, and set aside to cool.
2. In food processor, combine cooled kale, parsley, pumpkin seeds, garlic, salt, and pepper. Process until well incorporated and smooth.
3. Slowly stream in olive oil to further incorporate mixture. Scrape down sides with rubber spatula once or twice to ensure mixture is smooth and combined.
4. Set aside.

For the Assembly

1. Drain each portobello and place on a plate, gill-side up.
2. Spread ⅓ cup Kale Parsley Pesto on each portobello.
3. Top with Harvest Stuffing and serve.

PINTO BEAN BURGERS

MAKES 8 BURGERS

Transform your meat-loving friends with this mouthwatering vegan bean burger. This flavorful burger holds together well and can be made ahead. We've found they keep well in the freezer, and that freezing actually improves their consistency.

The patty is hearty and satisfying. Filled with a variety of vegetables and spices, it is a substantial recipe. We recommend that you make as many patties as you believe you might use over a month because they're easier to make in bulk.

FOR THE BURGERS

1 cup diced red onion
2 cloves garlic, minced
1 teaspoon salt
1 tablespoon sunflower oil
½ cup diced tomatoes
Juice of 1 lime
½ teaspoon smoked paprika
1 teaspoon chipotle powder
1 teaspoon turmeric
1 teaspoon chili powder
1 teaspoon ground cumin

1 teaspoon cayenne pepper
1 teaspoon pepper
2 cups cooked pinto beans
1½ cups diced
or crumbled tempeh
½ cup diced sweet potato
2 stalks celery, diced small
1 zucchini, diced small
¼ cup nutritional yeast
2 tablespoons miso
2 tablespoons ground flaxseed
½ cup masa

Parchment paper
Focaccia Buns (page 68) or
Whole Wheat Burger Buns
(page 69)
2 avocados, sliced
2 tomatoes, sliced
Lettuce, for garnish

FOR THE PICKLED ONIONS

2 red onions, thinly sliced
½ cup agave syrup
½ cup brown rice vinegar

For the Burgers

1. In a sauté pan, sauté onion, garlic, and salt in oil over medium heat until translucent, about 5–7 minutes.
2. Add in tomatoes. Cook 3 more minutes.
3. Add lime juice and all spices. Stir to combine.
4. Let mixture cool for 20–30 minutes and set aside.
5. Once cool, combine mixture with pinto beans, tempeh, sweet potato, celery, zucchini, nutritional yeast, miso, flaxseed, and masa in large mixing bowl and knead with hands for about 1 minute. Let mixture chill in fridge for at least 20–30 minutes, or up to 2 hours.
6. Preheat oven to 350 degrees.
7. Form patties using ½-cup balls of mixture (use oiled ½-cup scoop or ½-cup measuring cup). Place patties on baking sheets lined

Recipe continued on next page . . .

with parchment paper.

8. Bake for 15 minutes. Check for firmness and then flip. Bake for 10–15 minutes longer, until golden brown. Alternatively, cook on stove top using a frying pan and spray oil to prevent sticking. Cook each side until firm, about 3–5 minutes.

9. Store in refrigerator for up to 5 days. Store in freezer for up to 1 month.

10. Serve on Focaccia Buns or Whole Wheat Burger Buns with pickled red onions, avocado, tomato, and lettuce.

For the Pickled Onions

1. Combine all ingredients and let marinate for at least 1 hour before serving.

WILD MUSHROOM AND SPINACH ROULADE

MAKES 2–3 ROLLS; 3–5 SERVINGS

This is an attractive and festive dish for the holidays. Predominately made with whole foods, the roulade "burns well," meaning it will not leave you and your guests feeling bloated and bilious as do many traditional holiday dinners. We serve this dish with either green beans or roasted Brussels sprouts and wild rice.

Serve with sautéed greens for color.

FOR THE DRIED MUSHROOMS

1 cup dried porcini mushrooms (see note)

1 tablespoon minced garlic

½ cup white wine

½ cup Ravens All-Purpose Vegetable Stock (page 163) or store-bought vegan broth

FOR THE WILD MUSHROOM MIXTURE

2 cups sliced fresh wild mushrooms such as chanterelles or hedgehogs (see note)

1 yellow or white onion, thinly sliced into half-moons

2 shallots, thinly sliced into half-moons

½ tablespoon white pepper

¼ teaspoon salt

1 tablespoon olive oil

½ bunch chives, minced (about ¼ cup)

1 tablespoon minced fresh thyme

1 tablespoon dried thyme

½ teaspoon green pepper

1 teaspoon golden balsamic vinegar

2 tablespoons pinot gris or comparable white wine

½ tablespoon mirin

½ teaspoon ume plum vinegar

4 cups chopped spinach

FOR THE PORT WINE REDUCTION

1 (750-milliliter) bottle inexpensive organic port wine

1–2 tablespoons maple syrup, or to taste

FOR THE ASSEMBLY

1 (16-ounce) package whole wheat fillo dough (we use Fillo Factory Organic Whole Wheat Fillo Dough)

Olive oil

Paprika

For the Dried Mushrooms

1. Combine dried mushrooms, garlic, white wine, and vegetable stock in a saucepan and cook 15–20 minutes, until mushrooms are soft.
2. Allow to cool, then cut into a medium dice and set aside.

For the Wild Mushroom Mixture

1. In a large sauté pan, sauté mushrooms, white onion, shallots, white pepper, salt, and olive oil over medium heat until slightly brown and soft, about 7–10 minutes.
2. Add chives, fresh and dried thyme, green pepper, and balsamic vinegar, tossing lightly until evenly distributed.
3. Deglaze pan with pinot gris, mirin, and ume plum vinegar.
4. Add the dried mushroom mixture to the sautéed sliced wild mushrooms.

5. Fold in chopped spinach while mixture is still warm. Set aside.

For the Port Wine Reduction

1. Place port wine in pot over medium heat and bring to a simmer. Stir occasionally and reduce to half, about 10–12 minutes. Cool.
2. If mixture is too thin, heat for 5–10 minutes longer to further reduce.
3. If mixture is too sour, incrementally add in maple syrup to taste at the end of the cooking process.

For the Assembly

1. Preheat oven to 350 degrees.
2. Brush a sheet of fillo dough with olive oil and sprinkle with paprika. Repeat for a total of 6 layers. Repeat to make 1 or 2 more rolls.
3. Place cooled mushroom mixture on fillo dough and smooth flat over three-fourths of the dough surface. The top one-fourth will be used to seal the roll.
4. Roll fillo dough into a very tight roll and spray the area that does not have the mushroom mixture with spray oil to seal the roll.
5. Bake rolls on a baking sheet for 15–20 minutes, or until golden brown. Slice each roll into five ¾- to 1-inch rounds. Garnish dish with the Port Wine Reduction.
6. Rolls can be wrapped in plastic and frozen for up to 2 months.

Porcini Mushroom Note: Most dried mushrooms will work, but porcini have the best flavor for this dish. You can use shiitake or matsutake mushrooms if you can't find porcinis.

Wild Mushroom Note: Other wild mushrooms, such as oyster mushrooms or trumpet mushrooms, may work, but the texture is much chewier, so cut the mushrooms smaller. Another good alternative would be enoki mushrooms.

MUSHROOM PESTO AND SUN-DRIED TOMATO BURGER

MAKES 10 LARGE BURGERS

This is a burger that belongs in a bun. The flavor comes from the tannins
in the mushrooms, pesto, and peppers; the structure from the walnuts and rice;
and it is all held together by flax meal, oats, and rice flour. Properly sealed,
you can freeze the patties for those times you have the urge for a hamburger.
Simply thaw and heat on a grill or griddle.
It's Joan's favorite burger!

FOR THE MUSHROOM PESTO

½ cup walnuts

2 cups chopped basil leaves
(replace 1 cup of basil with
kale if desired)

½ cup nutritional yeast

8 cloves garlic, raw or roasted

1 tablespoon chickpea miso

¼ teaspoon white pepper

Salt to taste

Juice of ½ lemon

2 tablespoons olive oil

FOR THE BURGER

1 pound portobello or cremini
mushrooms, diced medium

1 yellow onion, diced medium

1 jalapeño or serrano pepper,
seeded and diced

1 tablespoon olive oil

¾ cup sun-dried tomato
pieces, soaked in water for
1 hour and drained

3 cups cooked short-grain
brown rice

Salt and pepper to taste

½ cup gluten-free oats

½ cup chopped walnuts

¼ cup hemp seeds

2 tablespoons ground flaxseeds

1 cup brown rice flour

Parchment paper

For the Mushroom Pesto

1. Process the walnuts in a food processor by pulsing.
2. Add remaining ingredients and process. Add water if needed to get the mixture moving.
3. Adjust and season with more salt and lemon if desired.

For the Burger

1. Sauté mushrooms, onion, and jalapeño with olive oil in a sauté pan over medium heat for 7–10 minutes, until mushrooms and jalapeño have darkened and softened. The onions will be slightly browned. Set aside and let cool.
2. Add half the mushroom and onion mixture, half the sun-dried tomatoes, half the rice, 1½ cups Mushroom Pesto, and salt and pepper to a food processor and pulse until well combined, but some chunks remain. Do not overprocess!
3. Transfer mixture to bowl and add the remaining mushroom and onion mixture, sun-dried tomatoes, and cooked rice.
4. Add the oats, walnuts, hemp seeds, and flaxseeds and combine. Add the brown rice flour a little at a time until the consistency is not sticky, but can easily be formed into a ball. Refrigerate mixture for about 20 minutes or overnight.
5. Preheat oven to 350 degrees.
6. Form patties using ½ cup of the burger mixture for each patty. Form into a ball with oiled hands or 4-ounce ice cream scoop, and place onto a baking sheet lined with parchment paper.
7. Using an oiled palm, press patties down to form round disks.
8. Test bake one burger before making the entire batch. Burger should be crisp on the outside and cooked all the way through. It should not be gooey in the middle.
9. Bake for 12 minutes, then flip over, and cook for an additional 12–15 minutes. The patties are done when they have browned and are slightly crisp on the outside.
10. Serve burgers on toasted buns.

MOUSSAKA

10 SERVINGS

Moussaka is a classic Greek dish traditionally made with lamb and eggplant. Mendocino County is known for its lamb, and we find them beautiful romping with their mothers. We want them to continue romping, and so we use zucchini and spices instead of lamb to complete the dish. The flavors are uniquely Greek, rich, and aromatic.

We serve Moussaka with Dolmas (page 117), Quinoa Tabbouleh (page 132), and brown and green lentils cooked in tomato puree.

Preparation Note: The Moussaka should be prepared the day before serving and allowed to set overnight in the refrigerator in a springform pan.

FOR THE VEGETABLE LAYERS

3 large eggplants

2 tablespoons plus 3½ teaspoons salt, divided

Spray oil or ¼ cup olive oil, divided

1 tablespoon white pepper

4 zucchini

1 tablespoon Italian herbs

2 red bell peppers

2 green bell peppers

2 large yellow onions

1 tablespoon basil

4 tomatoes

1 tablespoon chopped fresh parsley

1 pound Yukon Gold potatoes

FOR THE LENTILS

1 cup cubed zucchini

2 teaspoons sunflower oil, divided

1 cup chopped white or yellow onion

4 cups Ravens All-Purpose Vegetable Stock (page 163) or store-bought vegan broth

2 cups brown/green lentils, soaked for 20 minutes or overnight and drained

1 cup tomato puree or crushed tomatoes

¼ cup tomato paste

3 cloves garlic, minced

1 teaspoon ground cinnamon

1 teaspoon onion powder

1 teaspoon garlic powder

¼ teaspoon ground allspice

¼ teaspoon ground cloves

Salt and pepper to taste

6 cups spinach

FOR THE SESAME DILL SAUCE

½ cup white sesame seeds, soaked for 1 hour and drained

2 cloves garlic, chopped

¼ cup water

1 teaspoon salt

Juice of 2 lemons

4 tablespoons olive oil

Agave syrup to taste (approximately 1 teaspoon)

3 tablespoons dried dill or 1 bunch (about 4½ ounces) fresh dill, finely chopped

FOR THE ASSEMBLY

Spray oil

1 batch Cashew Béchamel (page 81)

For the Vegetable Layers

1. Preheat oven to 425 degrees.
2. Peel and slice eggplant into ½-inch-thick rounds and "sweat" by spreading 2 tablespoons of the salt over the slices and allowing to sit for 30–60 minutes.

Recipe continued on next page . . .

3. Wash and dry eggplant rounds, then coat with spray oil or 3 tablespoons of the olive oil and white pepper.
4. Place slices on a hot grill and grill each side for 1–2 minutes. Set aside.
5. Thinly slice zucchini and toss with 1 teaspoon of the salt and Italian herbs. Spread on baking sheet.
6. Roast for 10–15 minutes, until tender. Gently remove from pan and set aside, leaving oven on.
7. Slice red and green bell peppers ½ inch thick.
8. Slice the onions into half-moons and toss with peppers, basil, and 1 teaspoon of the salt. Spread on baking sheet. Roast for 10–15 minutes, until tender and browned. Carefully remove from the pan and set aside, leaving oven on.
9. Slice tomatoes 1 inch thick and toss with ½ teaspoon of the salt and fresh parsley. Spread on baking sheet. Roast in oven for 10 minutes. Gently remove from pan and set aside, leaving oven on.
10. Slice potatoes ½ inch thick on a mandoline. Coat slices with spray oil or remaining 1 tablespoon olive oil and remaining 1 teaspoon salt. Place in a sheet pan and roast for 15 minutes until soft, not crisp. Set aside.

For the Lentils

1. In sauté pan over medium heat, sauté zucchini in 1 teaspoon of the oil until they turn golden, about 10 minutes. Set aside.
2. In a sauté pan over medium heat, cook onion in 1 teaspoon of the oil until it begins to brown, about 5–7 minutes. Set aside.
3. Bring stock to a boil in a heavy-duty pot. Add lentils, tomatoes, tomato paste, and spices and return to a boil. Reduce heat to low and simmer for 1–2 hours, until liquid is mostly absorbed and lentils are very soft. Turn off heat.
4. Fold in spinach, zucchini, and onion.
5. Cool the mixture in the fridge.

For the Sesame Dill Sauce

1. Place sesame seeds in a high-speed blender. Add garlic, water, salt, and lemon juice, and blend.
2. Keeping the blender running, stream in olive oil and blend until smooth.
3. Sweeten to taste with agave.
4. Place sesame mixture in a bowl. With spatula, fold in dill.

For the Assembly

1. Preheat oven to 350 degrees.
2. Make sure that all of the vegetables are well drained. If they have too much water content, the dish will be watery and have trouble sticking together.
3. Prepare a springform pan by lightly spraying with oil.
4. Layer potatoes on the bottom of the pan, slightly overlapping, to create your first layer.
5. Add one layer of eggplant atop the potatoes. Then place ½ cup of the Cashew Béchamel on top of the eggplant.
6. Add layers of zucchini, bell peppers, onions, then tomatoes, and finish with a top layer of eggplant. On the very top of all of layers, add all the remaining cooled Cashew Béchamel (this final layer will be about ¾ inch thick).
7. Bake on the top rack of oven with a sheet pan underneath to catch any overflow, for 20–25 minutes, or until top layer is brown. Cool and refrigerate overnight before cutting the slices.
8. To serve, reheat in a 350-degree oven for 5–8 minutes. Warm the lentils. Place warm lentils on a plate, then set a slice of the Moussaka on the lentils. Garnish with a drizzle of Sesame Dill Sauce.

DESSERTS

Desserts are important. Their ingredients stimulate the release of endorphins, providing a sense of well-being, aiding digestion, and ensuring that we receive the greatest nourishment from the food we have eaten. Of course, if eating dessert engenders a guilty feeling, we negate the beneficial aspects. Understanding this, desserts at The Ravens range from fruit sorbets to mega-calorie specialties—so we have something for those who want the dessert without the guilt and something for those who joyfully splurge during a special dinner. We selected our favorite desserts for this book.

Note: For sweeteners we use maple syrup, agave, and vegan sugar. The first two are almost always vegan. Cane sugar, however, is often filtered through charred animal bones that have been imported, so if you use cane sugar, look for brands that are labeled vegan. Beet sugar is vegan, so it's a safe option to use.

BASIC SORBET

MAKES 3 CUPS

We make a variety of sorbets every week using the bounty of fruit we have access to, living on California's north coast. We've used huckleberries, blackberries, raspberries, strawberries, cherries, and so many more. We freeze the fruit so we can use it in sorbets throughout the year.

---

4 cups seasonal fresh or frozen fruit

Juice of 1 lemon

¾ cup agave syrup

1 tablespoon arrowroot powder (optional; see note)

Procedure for Frozen Fruit

1. If using frozen fruit or fruit with a high water content, combine all ingredients, including arrowroot, in a large saucepan and let simmer over medium heat until mixture thickens slightly, about 12 minutes.
2. Transfer the mixture to a high-speed blender and blend until completely smooth. If using raspberries or blackberries, strain the blended liquid through a chinois or cheesecloth to remove all seeds.
3. Add mixture to an ice cream maker and freeze for at least 1 hour, or until firm.

Procedure for Fresh Fruit

1. If using fresh fruit, add all ingredients except the arrowroot powder (you won't need it) to a high-speed blender and blend until smooth. Strain the liquid through a chinois or cheesecloth if the fruit contains a lot of seeds.
2. Add mixture to an ice cream maker and freeze for at least 1 hour, or until firm.

Arrowroot Note: Whether or not you need the arrowroot powder depends on the water content of the fruit you're using (for example, mango and berries may not need an additional thickener because they aren't watery fruits). Frozen fruit releases water when thawed and usually needs thickener.

PECAN TUILES

MAKES 24–32 TUILE COOKIES OR CUPS

We often use this as a sorbet cup. (Try serving with our Basic Sorbet, page 236.) It can also hold Vanilla Bean Ice Cream (page 254) with chocolate sauce, or serve as a fruit cup to make an otherwise simple dessert elegant.

---

2 cups pecans

2¼ cups brown rice flour

½ cup plus 1 tablespoon arrowroot powder

1½ cups agave syrup

1 cup plus 2 tablespoons brown rice syrup

½ cup plus 1 tablespoon coconut oil, melted

1½ tablespoons vanilla extract

Spray oil

1. In a food processor, pulse pecans until a fine powder is achieved.
2. In a bowl, combine pecan powder, brown rice flour, and arrowroot powder and stir until well mixed.
3. In separate bowl, whisk together agave, brown rice syrup, coconut oil, and vanilla extract until well combined.
4. Add wet mixture to the dry and mix well. Let batter sit for at least 15 minutes before baking.
5. Preheat oven to 350 degrees.
6. On a large sheet tray, lay down a silicone baking sheet. Spray sheet with oil. Pour batter onto sheet tray in 2-tablespoon increments (make sure to leave adequate space between each tuile, as each will spread and double in size).
7. Bake for 5 minutes, then rotate tray and cook for an additional 1 minute, or until golden brown. Do not overcook.
8. *Optional:* When you remove the baked tuiles from the oven, they will be soft. If carefully and quickly lifted from the tray and draped over juice glasses or the bottoms of muffin tins, they will form a cup shape when cool.

CANDY CAP MUSHROOM CRÈME BRÛLÉE

4-6 SERVINGS

Purely a joy to serve, this amazing dessert takes full advantage of the candy cap mushroom.

½ cup dried tightly packed candy cap mushrooms

1½ tablespoons agar agar flakes or 2¼ teaspoons agar agar powder

2½ cups almond milk, divided

1 (14-ounce) can coconut milk

¼ teaspoon salt

½ cup agave syrup

1 teaspoon vanilla extract

¼ cup tapioca starch

2 tablespoons cornstarch

Zest and juice of ½ lemon

4-6 teaspoons sugar

1. In medium saucepan, combine candy cap mushrooms, agar agar flakes, 2 cups of the almond milk, and coconut milk. Gently simmer for 20 minutes, until candy cap mushroom flavor infuses into the milk and agar agar dissolves. Do not let this mixture boil. Carefully strain out the mushrooms and return liquid to the saucepan.

2. Stir salt, agave, and vanilla extract into the saucepan with mushroom-infused mixture and cook over medium-low heat until well incorporated, about 5 minutes.

3. In separate bowl, combine tapioca starch, cornstarch, and remaining ½ cup almond milk to make a slurry. (Make sure the almond milk is cold so that clumps do not form.)

4. Slowly whisk slurry into mushroom-infused mixture to fully incorporate. Whisk for a minute until mixture starts to thicken. Once thickening has begun, use a wooden spoon to mix occasionally.

5. Cook mixture over low heat for another 10 minutes until it is thick like porridge. Add lemon zest and juice, and stir to combine.

6. Portion out ¾ cup (or desired amount) of mixture into 4–6 ramekins. (We use 8-ounce shallow brûlée ramekins.)

7. Cool and then chill in refrigerator for at least 4 hours for custards to firm.

8. Right before serving, sprinkle 1 teaspoon sugar evenly over each chilled custard.

9. Using an ignited kitchen torch, gently hover the flame over the sugar crystals. Move flame in a circular motion over the sugar until caramelized and golden brown.

VANILLA CRÈME BRÛLÉE

MAKES ABOUT 10–12 SERVINGS, DEPENDING ON RAMEKIN SIZE

Our "everyday" brûlée is part of our repertoire of dishes to amaze!

2½ (13.5-ounce) cans coconut milk

Seeds from 1 vanilla bean (see note)

1½ tablespoons agar agar flakes

2 cups almond milk

¼ cup cornstarch

¼ cup tapioca starch

¾ teaspoon salt

½ cup Frangelico (see note)

¼ cup agave syrup

1½ teaspoons vanilla extract

10–12 teaspoons sugar

1. In medium saucepan, combine coconut milk and vanilla bean seeds. Let sit for 5 minutes.

2. Meanwhile, add agar agar flakes and almond milk to another medium saucepan, and bring to a boil over medium-high heat. Reduce heat to a simmer and cook for 15 minutes, until flakes are dissolved.

3. After vanilla bean seeds have infused into the coconut milk, add cornstarch, tapioca starch, salt, Frangelico, agave, and vanilla extract to the mixture. Whisk over medium heat until thickened, about 10–12 minutes. Watch the mixture closely, making sure not to bring it to a boil.

4. When coconut milk is thickened and agar agar is completely dissolved in the almond milk, slowly whisk the agar agar mixture into the coconut milk mixture. Whisk for 2–3 minutes (mixture should be thick and creamy), then pour into ten to twelve 8-ounce brûlée ramekins.

5. Allow to cool at room temperature before storing in refrigerator.

6. Right before serving, sprinkle 1 teaspoon sugar evenly over each chilled custard.

7. Using an ignited kitchen torch, gently hover the flame over the sugar crystals. Move flame in a circular motion over the sugar until caramelized and golden brown.

Vanilla Bean Note: To split open the vanilla pod, gently break it open with a sharp paring knife. Then, using the back of the knife, scrape the vanilla seeds out of the pod.

Frangelico Note: You can substitute 2 teaspoons almond or hazelnut extract and ¼ cup water for the Frangelico.

CARROT CAKE

MAKES ONE 9-INCH ROUND CAKE AND 2½ CUPS FROSTING

This is the only carrot cake Jeff likes. It is simple but flavorful, leaving out the extra ingredients typical of carrot cake—no nuts, no raisins, no coconut, no pineapple. Our Carrot Cake is in no way a disguised fruitcake. And yet its recipe is often requested.

FOR THE CARROT CAKE

Parchment paper

Spray oil

2⅓ cups pastry flour or 10.8 ounces all-purpose flour (for best results, we use Giusto's Baker's Choice)

2 teaspoons ground cinnamon

1½ teaspoons baking powder

1 teaspoon baking soda

¾ teaspoon salt

½ teaspoon ground nutmeg

⅛ teaspoon ground allspice

¾ cup granulated sugar

1 cup apple juice

½ cup sunflower oil

½ cup maple syrup

2 teaspoons vanilla extract

2 cups grated carrot

FOR THE CARROT CAKE FROSTING

1 cup Earth Balance Organic Coconut Spread, cold

1½ cups Earth Balance Vegan Shortening Sticks, chilled and cut into small cubes

2 cups powdered sugar

1 tablespoon vanilla extract

For the Carrot Cake

1. Preheat oven to 350 degrees.
2. Line a round 9-inch cake pan with parchment paper and spray the parchment with oil.
3. In a large bowl, sift together flour, cinnamon, baking powder, baking soda, salt, nutmeg, and allspice.
4. In a medium bowl, whisk together granulated sugar, apple juice, sunflower oil, maple syrup, and vanilla extract.
5. Add wet mixture to flour mixture and stir until no large clumps remain.
6. Add grated carrot to the batter and stir in.
7. Pour batter into prepared cake pan and tap against countertop to remove any air bubbles.
8. Bake for about 25 minutes, until inserted toothpick removes cleanly.
9. Cool completely.
10. Carefully remove from pan.
11. Cover entire cake with Carrot Cake Frosting.

For the Carrot Cake Frosting

1. Whip Earth Balance Organic Coconut Spread with paddle attachment in a stand mixer.
2. Add Earth Balance shortening cubes to the whipped Coconut Spread, and whip until creamy.
3. Leaving the mixer running, sift powdered sugar 1 cup at a time into the Earth Balance mixture to remove any clumps.
4. Add vanilla extract, and continue whipping until the frosting has achieved spreading consistency.
5. Store in airtight container in fridge or freezer for up to 1 month.

CHOCOLATE GANACHE TART

MAKES TWO 9-INCH TARTS

This dessert has undergone a variety of transformations over the years. It is now a rich mint chocolate ganache. The mint was added in 2010. It is our single-most popular dessert.

We knew we had a "winner" when our diners would challenge us, "You gotta be kidding. It has to have dairy in it!" It doesn't.

FOR THE CRUST

2½ cups raw, unsalted almonds

2½ cups raw hazelnuts

½ cup cane sugar

⅓ cup cacao powder

½ tablespoon salt

¾ cup coconut oil, at room temperature or softened

1 tablespoon vanilla extract

¼ cup water
(or more as needed)

FOR THE GANACHE FILLING AND ASSEMBLY

1 (14-ounce) package Wildwood Sprouted Silken Tofu (if unavailable, use a firm silken tofu, about 13 ounces if not water packed)

1 cup plus 2 tablespoons unbleached cane sugar

Pinch of salt

1 cup water

1 tablespoon vanilla extract

2 teaspoons mint extract

1 cup semisweet vegan chocolate chips

For the Crust

1. Preheat oven to 350 degrees.
2. Finely grind almonds and hazelnuts in a food processor until they form a relatively smooth powder with some small chunks.
3. Add sugar, cacao powder, and salt. Using the pulse button, mix the ingredients.
4. Pour processed dry ingredients into a bowl and add coconut oil and vanilla. Toss, adding water incrementally until mixture sticks together.
5. Press into two 9-inch tart/quiche pans.
6. Bake for 10 minutes, until brown. Let cool completely.

For the Ganache Filling and Assembly

1. Place tofu, sugar, salt, water, vanilla extract, and mint extract into a large saucepan.
2. Mash tofu lightly into smaller pieces with potato masher or whisk.
3. Bring mixture to boil. Reduce heat and let simmer until liquid reduces and tofu turns light brown, 15–20 minutes.
4. Turn off heat, add chocolate chips, and mix until melted.
5. Place mixture in a high-speed blender and blend until smooth.
6. Pour into prebaked chocolate nut crust.
7. Refrigerate before serving.

Note: If leftover filling is refrigerated, it will stiffen. If so, you can melt it down over low heat or over a double boiler and pour into prebaked tart shell. It can be used as a treat or dessert on its own in a parfait glass, or warmed and poured over broken-up leftover chocolate cake.

CHOCOLATE CHIP COOKIES

MAKES 24 COOKIES

If you have ever stayed at the Stanford Inn, you know that we provide chocolate chip cookies for each night of your stay. You may also be one of many who has wished we had left more cookies in your room. Perhaps you may have ordered some to take home. The following is the recipe we use.

¼ cup Ener-G Egg Replacer (page 256)

½ cup plus 1 tablespoon water

1½ tablespoons vanilla extract

4 cups unbleached all-purpose flour

2 teaspoons baking soda

1½ cups Earth Balance Vegan Shortening Sticks, diced medium

1½ cups brown sugar

1½ cups granulated sugar

1 cup vegan semisweet chocolate chips

1. Preheat oven to 350 degrees.
2. Mix together egg replacer, water, and vanilla extract in a high-speed blender. Blend well and set aside.
3. In a large bowl, mix together flour and baking soda and set aside.
4. In the bowl of a stand mixer, cream together Earth Balance and both sugars. Add egg replacer mixture and whip until fluffy, scraping the bowl to incorporate all ingredients.
5. Stir flour mixture by hand into the Earth Balance mixture.
6. Stir in the chocolate chips.
7. Roll out dough into golf ball-size cookies and place on a greased baking sheet, about 5 inches apart.
8. Press each ball with the palm of your hand, making a flat cookie.
9. Bake for 12 minutes, or until cookies begin to brown.

PEACH HUCKLEBERRY COBBLER

MAKES SIX 4-INCH RAMEKINS

Cobblers are great desserts, and this is the one we like to serve in late summer.

We use huckleberries in this recipe, which are found virtually everywhere on the Mendocino coast. Most people don't know that the huckleberry is a more potent berry than the blueberry, promoting health, enhancing the immune system, and protecting our eyes. Another name for it is *bilberry*.

FOR THE COBBLER FILLING

4 ripe, peeled peaches, diced medium (approximately 3 cups)

1 cup huckleberries or blueberries

2 tablespoons cornstarch

¼ teaspoon salt

½ cup agave syrup

Juice and zest of 1 lemon

FOR THE COBBLER TOPPING

1 cup raw almonds

½ cup gluten-free oats

1 teaspoon ground cinnamon

¼ teaspoon salt

Pinch of ground nutmeg

½ cup maple syrup

For the Cobbler Filling

1. In a large mixing bowl, combine all ingredients and mix until evenly distributed.
2. Measure ½ cup of filling into six 4-inch ramekins. Set aside and prepare cobbler topping.

For the Cobbler Topping

1. Preheat oven to 350 degrees.
2. Add almonds to a food processor, and process until coarse, sandlike consistency is achieved.
3. Add oats and process for another 30–60 seconds until mixture is well combined, resembling smooth sand.
4. Add cinnamon, salt, nutmeg, and maple syrup and mix further to incorporate. Mixture will resemble sticky paste.
5. Divide cobbler topping among the 6 ramekins (about 2½ tablespoons per ramekin). Make sure to spread evenly so topping is well distributed.
6. Bake for 30 minutes, or until topping is golden brown and filling is slightly bubbling.

LEMON CUSTARD BARS

MAKES 18 BARS

Tart and delicious, this is a true treat. Both of our mothers served Lemon Custard Bars for dessert. We shared a love for the tart long before we met!

What's missing from this recipe, besides the considerable eggs found in conventional recipes, is the powdered sugar Jeff's mom used to sprinkle over her version. There is no discernable difference between the eggy original and this much healthier version.

FOR THE CRUST

2 cups raw walnuts
1 cup canola oil
3½ cups all-purpose flour
1 cup vegan sugar
1 teaspoon salt
1 teaspoon baking powder

FOR THE LEMON CUSTARD FILLING AND ASSEMBLY

¼ cup plus 2 tablespoons cornstarch
4 tablespoons agar agar powder or 4 ounces agar agar flakes
2 (13.6-ounce) cans coconut milk
1 cup agave syrup
Zest and juice of 6 lemons (Meyer lemon preferred)

For the Crust

1. Preheat oven to 350 degrees.
2. In a food processor, pulse walnuts until fine powder is achieved. Slowly stream in canola oil while processing to incorporate.
3. In a separate large bowl, combine flour, sugar, salt, and baking powder. Mix until well combined.
4. Add walnut mixture to the flour mixture and stir until well incorporated.
5. Press mixture into a lightly oiled 9 x 12-inch cake pan, covering the bottom and coming up about ¾ inch along the sides of the pan. Bake for 14 minutes.
6. Cool crust completely.

For the Lemon Custard Filling and Assembly

1. In a medium saucepan, combine all ingredients and simmer for 10 minutes until mixture thickens (and powders are dissolved), whisking constantly.
2. Pour contents into a high-speed blender and process until completely smooth.
3. Pour into prepared cooled crust.
4. Let cool before refrigerating, then serve chilled, cut into 2 x 3-inch bars.

PECAN TORTE

MAKES TWO 9-INCH TORTES

Pecan Torte is our most requested dessert recipe; diners love this sweet rendition of a Southern classic. We serve our version in a cylindrical shape. We assemble the tart, first stuffing the crust into a 3-inch metal cylinder, followed by the pecan mixture. When we serve it, we push the torte out of the cylinder onto a plate, and then top with Vanilla Bean Ice Cream (page 254).

Most homes do not have cooking cylinders. We suggest you use two 9-inch tart pans with removable bottoms. "Two," you ask? After you try it, you'll understand why.

FOR THE PECAN TORTE CRUST

2 cups raw, unsalted almonds (raw, unsalted walnuts can be used if almonds are unavailable or if you prefer)

1 cup sunflower oil

3¼ cups whole wheat flour or gluten-free flour

1 cup brown sugar

1 teaspoon salt

1 teaspoon baking powder

FOR THE FILLING

3 cups pecans, lightly toasted

¼ teaspoon salt

1 cup maple syrup

½ cup brown rice syrup

1 tablespoon vanilla extract

¼ cup plus 2 tablespoons arrowroot powder

¼ cup plus 2 tablespoons almond milk

For the Pecan Torte Crust

1. Preheat oven to 350 degrees.
2. In a food processor, pulse almonds until fine powder is achieved.
3. Keeping the processor on, stream in sunflower oil until well incorporated.
4. Stop processing and add flour, brown sugar, salt, and baking powder to the almond mixture. Process until combined.
5. Remove from food processor and pour into large mixing bowl. Combine further using your hands (gloves should be worn), to make sure well incorporated.
6. Pat the crust into two 9-inch tart pans.
7. Bake for 15 minutes, remove from the oven, and cool completely.

For the Filling

1. Preheat oven to 350 degrees.
2. Combine pecans, salt, maple syrup, brown rice syrup, and vanilla extract in a large saucepan over low heat. Stir occasionally and do not allow mixture to come to a boil.
3. In separate bowl, combine arrowroot with almond milk and mix until arrowroot is fully dissolved.
4. Pour arrowroot mixture slowly into the pecan mixture. Continue to simmer over low heat until thickened (about 5 minutes).
5. Pour pecan mixture into prebaked crusts in tart pans.
6. Bake for 20–25 minutes and serve warm.

BANANA SPLIT

MAKES 1 SPLIT, 3½ CUPS VANILLA BEAN ICE CREAM,
4 CUPS STRAWBERRY ICE CREAM, AND 4 CUPS CHOCOLATE ICE CREAM

This dessert is just fun! It showcases our ice creams and our staff's desire to amaze every night. We watch them assemble this dish, smiling, while putting on the finishing touches. It is vegan, and it is joyful!

Note: Instructions for making the split components follow the general assemblage.

FOR THE ASSEMBLY

1 banana

1 scoop Vanilla Bean Ice Cream

1 scoop Strawberry Ice Cream

1 scoop Chocolate Ice Cream

Berry syrup (such as Starbucks Raspberry Syrup or Monin Organic Raspberry Syrup), for garnish

Vanilla syrup (such as Starbucks Vanilla Syrup or Monin Organic Vanilla Syrup), for garnish

Vegan chocolate syrup (such as Santa Cruz Organic Chocolate Syrup), for garnish

Coconut Whipped Cream, for garnish

Chocolate Almond Bark, for garnish

Toasted Coconut Sprinkles, for garnish

FOR THE VANILLA BEAN ICE CREAM

2 (14-ounce) cans coconut milk

¾ cup agave syrup

1 tablespoon vanilla extract

1 vanilla bean, cut in half lengthwise, and seeds scraped out of pod (reserve seeds and pod)

Pinch of salt

FOR THE STRAWBERRY ICE CREAM

1 cup hulled and chopped fresh or frozen strawberries

Pinch of salt

2 (14-ounce) cans coconut milk

¾ cup agave syrup

Juice of 1 lemon

FOR THE CHOCOLATE ICE CREAM

¾ cup semisweet vegan chocolate chips

Pinch of salt

2 (14-ounce) cans coconut milk

¾ cup agave syrup (or more to taste)

1 teaspoon vanilla extract

FOR THE COCONUT WHIPPED CREAM

2 (14-ounce) cans coconut milk

1 teaspoon vanilla

¾ cup vegan powdered sugar

FOR THE CHOCOLATE ALMOND BARK

½ cup semisweet vegan chocolate chips

2 tablespoons almond pieces or whole almonds

FOR THE TOASTED COCONUT SPRINKLES

1 (8-ounce) package unsweetened shredded coconut

For the Assembly

1. Keeping the banana in the peel, cut it lengthwise, and split it open in a large, long boat bowl.
2. Add the ice cream scoops to the split in the banana.
3. Top with berry, vanilla, and chocolate sauces.

Recipe continued on next page . . .

4. Top with Coconut Whipped Cream.
5. Finish with Chocolate Almond Bark and Toasted Coconut Sprinkles.

For the Vanilla Bean Ice Cream

1. In a medium saucepan, combine all ingredients including vanilla pods and seeds over low heat.
2. Cook for about 10 minutes to infuse the mixture with the vanilla bean.
3. Remove vanilla bean pod, and add the mixture to an ice cream maker. Follow ice cream maker's instructions.

For the Strawberry Ice Cream

1. If using frozen strawberries, thaw them out in saucepan over low heat. If you're using fresh strawberries, skip to next step.
2. Add strawberries and all remaining ingredients to a high-speed blender and blend until completely smooth
3. Add mixture to ice cream maker. Follow ice cream maker's instructions.

For the Chocolate Ice Cream

1. Add all ingredients to a saucepan and cook over low heat until chocolate is melted. Do not bring to a boil.
2. Add mixture to ice cream maker. Follow ice cream maker's instructions.

For the Coconut Whipped Cream

1. Chill canned coconut milk.
2. Carefully open and remove congealed cream from the top. Leave the watery coconut milk in the can.
3. Put coconut cream in a chilled bowl with vanilla and begin beating, slowly adding sugar until well mixed. Store in the refrigerator.

For the Chocolate Almond Bark

1. Melt the chocolate chips in a double boiler.
2. Pour the melted chips over a greased baking sheet or silicone baking mat.
3. Sprinkle almonds onto the chocolate. Cool.
4. Once cooled, chill in the refrigerator to harden for 2 hours or longer.
5. Remove hardened chocolate from the pan or silicone baking mat. Break bark into large chunks with your hands.

For the Toasted Coconut Sprinkles

1. Preheat oven to 350 degrees.
2. Spread a single layer of shredded coconut on baking sheet.
3. Toast the coconut in the oven until golden brown, approximately 10 minutes.

PANTRY BASICS

The following recipes are the building blocks of many of our dishes. Some stand on their own, like those for "Refried" Pinto Beans (page 269) and Mexican Rice (page 268), and others, like the Flax "Egg" (page 256) are essential for creating other dishes.

FLAX "EGG"

Works well in baking (for muffins, pancakes, and cookies) as a binder.

1 tablespoon freshly ground flaxseed

3 tablespoons water

1. Whisk together flax and water in a small bowl until foamy.
2. Cool in refrigerator for approximately 5 minutes, then use immediately.

ENER-G EGG REPLACER

MAKES 1 EGG REPLACEMENT

Best used in general baking.

1 tablespoon Ener-G

2 tablespoons water

1. Whisk together Ener-G and water in a small bowl to create a slurry.
2. Use immediately.

HERBED CHICKPEA CREPE

MAKES ABOUT 6 CREPES

We originally used this recipe with silken tofu and plenty of turmeric to replace
our egg omelet. Then along came the American fear of gluten. We were happily
producing non-gluten savory pancakes and we thinned them using soymilk rather
than tofu and began stuffing them with everything from wild mushrooms to squash.
Versatile, these crepes can help create a very sophisticated breakfast or dinner.

---

1 cup organic soymilk or 1 pound silken tofu (see note)

¼ teaspoon salt

¼ teaspoon pepper

¼ teaspoon turmeric

½ cup chickpea flour

1½ tablespoons arrowroot

½ teaspoon finely chopped chives

½ teaspoon finely chopped Italian parsley

1. In a blender, blend soymilk, salt, pepper, and turmeric until smooth.
2. Mix in chickpea flour, arrowroot, and herbs.
3. Cook as an ordinary crepe in a crepe pan, lightly coated in oil: Heat pan and pour in ¼–⅓ cup batter and create a very thin layer by immediately tilting and spreading the batter over the pan's surface. Cook until the edges begin to dry out and pull from the pan. Gently lift the crepe and flip onto the uncooked side and cook another minute.

Soymilk Note: If you wish for a more omelet-like crepe, replace the soymilk with 1 pound silken tofu, or about 1⅓ (14-ounce) boxes, and add an extra ¼ teaspoon turmeric, 2 tablespoons nutritional yeast, 2 tablespoons olive oil, and 2 cloves garlic in the first step. This creates a thicker crepe with a more egglike texture.

RAVENS VEGAN CASHEW CHEESE

MAKES ABOUT 4½ POUNDS

This "cheese" melts! And it is complements many dishes, such as the Ravens Reuben (page 193; we like a bit of alliteration). We keep it on hand in large batches. Any extra can be frozen.

The turmeric provides more than color. This root's substantial health benefits include protecting the brain, reversing beta-amyloid plaque associated with Alzheimer's disease, and regenerating brain stem cells.

2½ cups raw cashews

1 cup nutritional yeast

1 tablespoon turmeric

4 teaspoons onion powder

3–5 teaspoons pink Himalayan sea salt to taste

¼ teaspoon garlic powder

7 cups soymilk or any dairy-free milk

4 tablespoons agar agar powder

1 cup sunflower oil or olive oil

⅓ cup miso paste (you can use any flavor, but for milder cheese, white miso works best)

4 tablespoons golden balsamic vinegar

½ teaspoon ume plum vinegar

OPTIONAL INGREDIENTS FOR DIFFERENT CHEESE FLAVORS

Sun-dried tomatoes and rosemary

Smoked sea salt

Dried sage and nutmeg

White, green, or black pepper

1. In food processor, pulse cashews into a fine powder. Do not over-process or the nuts will start to turn into nut butter.

2. Add nutritional yeast, turmeric, onion powder, sea salt, and garlic powder to the cashews. Sparingly pulse to blend ingredients.

3. Combine soymilk and agar agar flakes in a large saucepan and bring to a boil over high heat. Whisk until the mixture thickens. Turn down the heat and let simmer for 5–10 minutes, until agar agar dissolves. Decrease heat to low and whisk 1–2 more minutes until smooth. Remove from heat and let cool for 1–2 minutes, but not too long, or agar agar will set.

4. Turn on the food processor, and pour agar agar and soy mixture into the processor while it's running. Process for 2 minutes, and then add oil, miso paste, golden balsamic vinegar, and ume plum vinegar. Taste and adjust for salt.

5. Add any extra optional ingredients and process to change the flavor of the cheese.

6. Pour mixture into a lightly oiled 9 x 9-inch cake pan, and let set at room temperature for 15 minutes. Cover, then let set in fridge for 15 more minutes before serving. Cheese will keep for up to a week in the refrigerator. Freeze in small batches for up to 3 months for future use.

TOFU RICOTTA

MAKES 2 CUPS

This is absolutely versatile, and lighter and definitely healthier than traditional ricotta. Tofu is generally easier to find than the hemp required for the Hemp Ricotta (page 266).

---

1 pound firm tofu

2 tablespoons nutritional yeast (optional)

1 teaspoon salt

1 teaspoon fresh chopped thyme

6–8 fresh basil leaves

½ cup orange juice

Zest and juice of 2 lemons

2 tablespoons olive oil

1. Combine all ingredients in food processor and process until smooth and creamy texture is achieved. Do not overprocess the mixture or will become too smooth, and even watery.
2. Refrigerate for up to 3 days.

STANDARD SOUR CRÈME

MAKES 1¾ CUPS

We have to admit, we rarely use sour crème, but it is a transition condiment on the road to a whole-food diet. And that's why we make and use it at The Ravens. However, we don't use it at home, unless we are entertaining.

We use this vegan sour crème to help allure those who haven't figured out the advantages, and experienced the joy, of living on a plant-based, whole-food diet.

---

1 (14-ounce) package Wildwood Sprouted Silken Tofu or 1 (13-ounce) box other firm silken tofu

2 tablespoons nutritional yeast

1½ teaspoons salt

Juice of 1 lemon

1 teaspoon white wine vinegar or brown rice vinegar

1 teaspoon agave syrup

1. Combine all ingredients in a high-speed blender and puree until smooth.
2. Season with additional salt or lemon juice to desired taste.

TANGY SOUR CRÈME

MAKES 1¾ CUPS

This sour crème can be used as a base dressing in potato salad or coleslaw. For those of us who like Thousand Island dressing over a wedge of head lettuce, re-create it by adding a small amount of ketchup and drained pickle relish to this recipe.

---

1 (14-ounce) package Wildwood Sprouted Silken Tofu or 1 (13-ounce) box other firm silken tofu

3 tablespoons nutritional yeast

1 teaspoon dry mustard powder

1 teaspoon salt or to taste

2 tablespoons apple cider vinegar

1 tablespoon fresh lemon juice

1 tablespoon brown rice syrup

1. Combine all ingredients in a high-speed blender and puree until smooth.
2. Season with additional salt or lemon juice to desired taste.

Standard Sour Crème (back) and Tangy Sour Crème (front)

SHIITAKE BACON

MAKES ½–¾ CUP

The salty robust taste of bacon is easily reproduced with shiitake mushrooms. Use Shiitake Bacon on salads, atop roasted vegetables, and just in a bowl for nibbling. This recipe is easily adjusted by varying the amount of shiitake mushrooms.

8 cups shiitake mushrooms, stemmed

½ cup olive oil

Smoked paprika or smoked sea salt (if using the smoked sea salt, use less plain salt) to taste

Approximately 2 teaspoons salt

1. Preheat oven to 350 degrees.
2. Toss mushrooms lightly in oil and sprinkle with paprika and salt.
3. Spread out on sheet tray, and bake until crispy, approximately 30 minutes.

HEMP RICOTTA

MAKES 3 CUPS

Our ricotta of choice, this is a whole-food ricotta that can replace traditional ricotta in any recipe you're using. Stuff it in ravioli, add it to salads, or use it with campanelle or other shaped pasta, as a dip or spread on crostini, on pizza, or as the filling in our Eggplant Cannelloni (page 192).

Keeps for up to 7 days in the refrigerator, or 1 month in the freezer.

---

2 cups hemp seeds

2 tablespoons nutritional yeast

½ tablespoon salt

½–1 teaspoon white miso paste

½ teaspoon white pepper

½ cup Ravens All-Purpose Vegetable Stock (page 163) or store-bought vegan broth

½ cup water

2 tablespoons olive oil

Juice of 1 lemon

½ tablespoon golden balsamic vinegar

1 teaspoon ume plum vinegar

1 tablespoon dried or chopped fresh basil

1 tablespoon chopped fresh chives

1 tablespoon chopped fresh thyme

1 tablespoon dried or chopped fresh oregano or marjoram

1. Add all ingredients except the herbs to a food processor and blend until smooth.
2. Fold in herbs with a spoon.

   Note: If using frozen ricotta in a recipe, when thawing, re-blend or mix well with whisk.

MEXICAN RICE

6 SERVINGS

We use this recipe in a variety of dishes. It's flavorful and filling.

½ yellow onion, diced small

2 teaspoons olive oil

2 cups long-grain brown rice

1 small jalapeño, seeded and minced

2 cloves garlic, minced

1 tablespoon paprika

2 teaspoons salt

1½ teaspoons ground cumin

4 cups boiling water

¼ cup roughly chopped cilantro

1. In a medium sauté pan, sauté onion in olive oil over medium heat until soft and lightly browned, about 8 minutes.
2. Add rice and toast with the onion for 2–5 minutes, until well coated, stirring often.
3. Transfer rice and onion to a large bowl and toss with jalapeño, garlic, paprika, salt, and cumin.
4. Combine rice mixture and boiling water in a medium saucepan on the stove top. Simmer over low heat for 45 minutes, or until all the liquid is absorbed.
5. After rice has been cooking for about 30 minutes, mix in the cilantro.

STANFORD INN BLACK BEANS

MAKES ABOUT 4 CUPS

Our black beans can serve as a basic ingredient in many other dishes. You can serve black beans with melted Ravens Vegan Cashew Cheese (page 259), with Salsa Cruda (page 87), covered with Mexican-Spiced Tofu Scramble (page 58), or prepared in any of your favorite ways. Guests often ask us to combine our beans with a bowl of house potatoes smothered in vegan cheese and salsa for a really special treat.

If you use canned black beans, be sure to rinse them to remove the excess starch.

1 tablespoon finely chopped garlic

½ cup finely chopped cilantro

1 teaspoon chili powder

1 teaspoon ground cumin

¼ teaspoon ground black pepper

Salt to taste

2 cups dried black beans, soaked overnight and rinsed and drained

1. Combine garlic, cilantro, chili powder, cumin, pepper, and salt in a food processor fitted with a metal blade. Pulse until ingredients are well combined.
2. Place beans in a large pot and cover with water by 3 inches. Bring to a boil. Reduce heat, add garlic mixture, and simmer, covered, until tender, about 1 hour, continually checking water level.
3. When beans are tender, add salt to taste and set aside to cool.
4. Refrigerate after beans have reached room temperature.
5. Black beans will freeze well for up to 4 weeks.

"REFRIED" PINTO BEANS

4 SERVINGS (ROUGHLY ½ CUP PER SERVING)

Lardless refried beans. Quite easy to make, these beans are a healthy take on a Mexican classic.

1 cup dried pinto beans, soaked overnight (see note)

1 (3-inch) piece kombu

1½ teaspoons salt, divided

4 cups water

1. Drain beans from soaking liquid and rinse well.
2. Combine beans, kombu, 1 teaspoon of the salt, and water in large saucepan and bring to a boil over high heat.
3. Turn heat down and simmer until beans are very soft, about 1 hour.
4. Drain beans, reserving cooking liquid. Discard kombu piece.
5. Mash beans with the remaining ½ teaspoon salt, adding liquid as necessary to avoid beans becoming dry and crusty.

Beans Note: Canned pinto beans will work well, too. If using canned beans, make sure they are very soft. If they're firm, pour into a pot and cook until softened. Reserve the liquid, but wash the beans of excess starch.

METRIC CONVERSION CHARTS

MEASUREMENT GUIDE

ABBREVIATION KEY	
tsp	teaspoon
tbsp	tablespoon
dsp	dessert spoon
U.S. STANDARD—U.K.	
¼ tsp	¼ tsp (scant)
½ tsp	½ tsp (scant)
¾ tsp	½ tsp (rounded)
1 tsp	¾ tsp (slightly rounded)
1 tbsp	2½ tsp
¼ cup	¼ cup minus 1 dsp
⅓ cup	¼ cup plus 1 tsp
½ cup	⅓ cup plus 2 dsp
⅔ cup	½ cup plus 1 dsp
¾ cup	½ cup plus 2 tbsp
1 cup	¾ cup and 2 dsp

OVEN TEMPERATURES: FAHRENHEIT (F)—CELSIUS (C)

250°F	120°C
275°F	135°C
300°F	150°C
325°F	160°C
350°F	180°C
375°F	190°C
400°F	200°C
425°F	220°C
450°F	230°C
475°F	245°C
500°F	260°C

ACKNOWLEDGMENTS

We want to express our deepest gratitude to the many people who have supported and worked with us in our pursuit of a style of innkeeping and restauranteering that is life enhancing for guests, diners, and staff.

This cookbook is the result of that collaborative effort, our co-creative kitchen. Everyone—prep cooks, dishwashers, creative directors, line cooks, dishwashers, lead chefs, servers, bussers, front desk staff, and gardeners—has helped create the recipes in this book.

Many of the recipes are inspired by their animal-based equivalents. More are inspired by the plants from which they are made. Our gardening staff has been inspiring from the very beginning, especially Dana Ecelberger, director emeritus of Big River Nurseries, and Jaime Jensen, who sees gardening as a path to mental and physical health. Lead landscaper Pedro Valenzuela introduced tomatillos to the kitchen and makes sure that we have fresh harvests as needed.

There are many people critical to the production of this book, not the least our editor, Heather Butterfield at BenBella Books, and both Lynda Layng and Metah Green, who tested and edited many of the recipes and corrected most. Sid Garza-Hillman coordinated all of it, working with our creative directors, cooks, chefs, and most importantly, a camera. He photographed many of the images that illustrate this book.

Living on the edge of North America as we do, people come and go in a rural restaurant's kitchen. One of those for whom we are especially grateful is a former intern who became head chef, Barry Horton. Barry came to us to fulfill internship requirements for the culinary program at Le Cordon Bleu in Portland, Oregon. When his internship was completed, we hired him. He became a line cook and eventually our head chef and a vegan. Barry contributed not only to the development of recipes, but he also penetrated language barriers and demonstrated an extraordinary ability to teach. Some of his "students" eventually left to become chefs in other parts of the country. Barry moved to the San Francisco Bay Area, where he and his wife opened Sanctuary Bistro in Berkeley, California.

Over the years, our approach to cuisine has changed. We are deeply appreciative of those who helped us through these changes, in particular creative directors Sadhana Berkow Houghland and Sally Weston Owens. They and the teams they worked with were and are invaluable. Additionally, both Sadhana and Sally tested and "tweaked" many of our recipes, scaling them for home use.

The following is a partial list of those who have contributed to The Ravens over the years—some not necessarily a recipe, but a comment, a tweak, an insight that made the ordinary extraordinary. We are deeply grateful for the contributions of Merlyn Alvarado, Michael Barnhouse, Jeremy Baumgartner, Janie Blake, Dominica Catelli, Joel Comacho, Porsche Combash, Esteban Duran, Kyle Evans, Andrew Field, Rebecca Katz, Georgia Lane, Julie Liebenbaum, Gustavo Martinez, Ubaldo Meraz, Alberto (Betto) Navarro, James Neidhardt, German Rosales, Michael Rossetti, Ted Scharpnick, Amy Smith, Victoria Ward, and many more.

Not only have the "professionals" contributed, but also interns from a variety of culinary programs, especially the Natural Gourmet Institute in New York City. Resa Soloway, an intern, suggested wrapping sea palm in fillo. Other interns, including Rachel Clement and Caitlin Boyer, have become dessert specialists.

Thanks, too, to all those who are not listed but have had something to say regarding seasonings, textures, or presentations of a dish. And thank you especially to our children, who have had to put up with our long hours, our almost endless discussions, and too many trips up the hill to the restaurant to taste, tweak, and even cook.

Finally, thank you to our guests and diners whose support and feedback makes this all worthwhile.

ABOUT THE AUTHORS

Jeff and Joan Stanford moved to the north coast of California in 1980, when they discovered Mendocino. They converted a bare-bones motel into an American Automobile Association Four Diamond inn and eco-resort dedicated to living sustainably. Here, with their two young children, they raised, and continue to have, llamas, horses, swans, and rescued dogs and cats on a working organic farm and inn. Believing that personal transformation most easily begins in the kitchen, they opened The Ravens Restaurant as first vegetarian and then totally plant based. Knowing that they could not do it all, they developed a model of a co-creative kitchen. At The Ravens they encourage everyone—from servers to bussers, cooks to dishwashers—to taste and suggest changes to a dish or offer completely new dishes.

Both Jeff and Joan are active in promoting healthy life choices and created the Mendocino Center for Living Well to offer classes from Creative Playshops to cooking and experiences from wildlife river tours to mushroom foraging to both the community and the inn's guests.

ONLINE RESOURCES

To see demonstrations of some of the recipes in this book, visit the
Cooking at Ravens! playlist on the Stanford Inn Eco-Resort YouTube channel:
www.youtube.com/channel/UC0nuasw5lvkBCZ0oLPkzpuQ

www.stanfordinn.com

 /stanford.inn.mendocino

 @EcoResort_CA

 @stanfordinnecoresort

VISIT THE RAVENS ONLINE:

www.ravensrestaurant.com

/Ravens.Restaurant

@Stanford_Ravens

INDEX

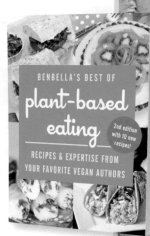